Copyright © 2025
Yatir Nitzany
All rights reserved.
ISBN-13: 978-1951244705
Printed in the United States of America

Also by Yatir Nitzany

Conversational Spanish Quick and Easy

Conversational French Quick and Easy

Conversational Italian Quick and Easy

Conversational Portuguese Quick and Easy

Conversational German Quick and Easy

Conversational Dutch Quick and Easy

Conversational Norwegian Quick and Easy

Conversational Danish Quick and Easy

Conversational Russian Quick and Easy

Conversational Ukrainian Quick and Easy

Conversational Bulgarian Quick and Easy

Conversational Polish Quick and Easy

Conversational Heew Quick and Easy

Conversational Yiddish Quick and Easy

Conversational Armenian Quick and Easy

Conversational Romanian Quick and Easy

Conversational Arabic Quick and Easy

CONVERSATIONAL LANGUAGES QUICK AND EASY SERIES
Germanic Series

German, Dutch, Danish, Norwegian, Swedish, and Yiddish

YATIR NITZANY

Foreword

About Myself

For many years I struggled to learn Spanish, and I still knew no more than about twenty words. Consequently, I was extremely frustrated. One day I stumbled upon this method as I was playing around with word combinations. Suddenly, I came to the realization that every language has a certain core group of words that are most commonly used and, simply by learning them, one could gain the ability to engage in quick and easy conversational Spanish.

I discovered which words those were, and I narrowed them down to three hundred and fifty that, once memorized, one could connect and create one's own sentences. The variations were and are *infinite*! By using this incredibly simple technique, I could converse at a proficient level and speak Spanish. Within a week, I astonished my Spanish-speaking friends with my newfound ability. The next semester I registered at my university for a Spanish language course, and I applied the same principles I had learned in that class (grammar, additional vocabulary, future and past tense, etc.) to those three hundred and fifty words I already had memorized, and immediately I felt as if I had grown wings and learned how to fly.

At the end of the semester, we took a class trip to San José, Costa Rica. I was like a fish in water, while the rest of my classmates were floundering and still struggling to converse. Throughout the following months, I again applied the same principle to other languages—French, Portuguese, Italian, and Arabic, all of which I now speak proficiently, thanks to this very simple technique.

This method is by far the fastest way to master quick and easy conversational language skills. There is no other technique that compares to my concept. It is effective, it worked for me, and it will work for you. Be consistent with my program, and you too will succeed the way I and many, many others have.

CONTENTS

Introduction to the Program 7
Memorization Made Easy 9

The German Language 10
Reading and Pronunciation in the German Language.... 12
The Program 13
Building Bridges 35
Other Useful Tools in the German Language 54

The Dutch Language 41
Reading and Pronunciation in the Dutch Language......... 43
The Program 44
Building Bridges 66
Other Useful Tools in the Dutch Language 71

The Danish Language 72
Reading and Pronunciation in the Danish Language......... 74
The Program 79
Building Bridges 101
Other Useful Tools in the Danish Language 106

The Norwegian Language 108
Reading and Pronunciation in the Norwegian Language .. 110
The Program 111
Building Bridges 133
Other Useful Tools in the Norwegian Language 138

The Swedish Language 104
Reading and Pronunciation in the Swedish Language 142
The Program 144
Building Bridges 166
Other Useful Tools in the Swedish Language 171

The Yiddish Language 172
The Program 174
Building Bridges 210
Other Useful Tools in the Yiddish Language 217

Congratulations Now You Are on Your Own............... 220
Note from the Author.. 222

Introduction to the Program

People often dream about learning a foreign language, but usually they never do it. Some feel that they just won't be able to do it while others believe that they don't have the time. Whatever your reason is, it's time to set that aside. With my new method, you will have enough time, and you will not fail. You will actually learn how to speak the fundamentals of the language—fluently in as little as a few days. Of course, you won't speak perfect German, Dutch, Danish, Norwegian, and Swedish at first, but you will certainly gain significant proficiency. For example, if you travel to any Germanic speaking countries, you will almost effortlessly be able engage in basic conversational communication with the locals in the present tense and you will no longer be intimidated by culture shock. It's time to relax. Learning a language is a valuable skill that connects people of multiple cultures around the world—and you now have the tools to join them.

How does my method work? I have taken twenty-seven of the most commonly used languages in the world and distilled from them the three hundred and fifty most frequently used words in any language. This process took three years of observation and research, and during that time, I determined which words I felt were most important for this method of basic conversational communication. In that time, I chose these words in such a way that they were structurally interrelated and that, when combined, form sentences. Thus, once you succeed in memorizing these words, you will be able to combine these words and form your own sentences. The words are spread over twenty pages. In fact, there are just nine basic words that will effectively build bridges, enabling you to speak in an understandable manner (please see Building Bridges at the end of every section). The words will also combine easily in sentences, for example, enabling you to ask simple questions, make basic statements, and obtain a rudimentary understanding of others' communications. I have also created Memorization-Made-Easy Techniques for this program in order to help with the memorization of the vocabulary.

My book is mainly intended for basic present tense vocal communication, meaning anyone can easily use it to "get by" linguistically while visiting a foreign country without learning the entire language. With practice, you will be 100 percent understandable to native speakers, which is your aim. One disclaimer: this is *not* a grammar book, though it does address minute and essential grammar rules (please see footnotes at the bottom of every page). Therefore, understanding complex sentences with obscure words in a foreign language is beyond the scope of this book.

People who have tried this method have been successful, and by the time you finish this book, you will understand and be understood in basic conversational language. This is the best basis to learn not only the Germanic languages but any languages. This is an entirely revolutionary, no-fail concept, and your ability to combine the pieces of the "language puzzle" together will come with *great* ease, especially if you use this program prior to beginning a foreign language class.

This is the best program that was ever designed to teach the reader how to become conversational. Other conversational programs will only teach you phrases. But this is the *only* program that will teach you how to create your *own* sentences for the purpose of becoming conversational.

Memorization Made Easy

There is no doubt the three hundred and fifty words in my program are the required essentials in order to engage in quick and easy basic conversation in any foreign language. However, some people may experience difficulty in the memorization. For this reason, I created Memorization Made Easy. This memorization technique will make this program so simple and fun that it's unbelievable! I have spread the words over the following twenty pages. Each page contains a vocabulary table of ten to fifteen words. Below every vocabulary box, sentences are composed from the words on the page that you have just studied. This aids greatly in memorization. Once you succeed in memorizing the first page, then proceed to the second page. Upon completion of the second page, go back to the first and review. Then proceed to the third page. After memorizing the third, go back to the first and second and repeat. And so on. As you continue, begin to combine words and create your own sentences in your head. Every time you proceed to the following page, you will notice words from the previous pages will be present in those simple sentences as well, because repetition is one of the most crucial aspects in learning any foreign language. Upon completion of your twenty pages, *congratulations*, you have absorbed the required words and gained a basic, quick-and-easy proficiency and you should now be able to create your own sentences and say anything you wish in these Germanic languages. This is a crash course in conversational German, Dutch, Danish, Norwegian, Swedish and Yiddish, and it works!

Conversational German Quick and Easy
The Most Innovative Technique to Learn the German Language

YATIR NITZANY

The German Language

The German language was first used during the Habsburg Empire in eastern Europe. Spoken by the common people of the time, the language was used more for economic trading and business. Though the Empire fell well over a hundred years ago, German remains one of ten most-common languages, as it is spoken by over one hundred and twenty million people. It is the official language of Germany, as well as one of twenty of the European Union. However, it is also spoken in various other countries, like Poland, Italy, Denmark, Belgium, Switzerland, and Austria. The language is spoken more frequently by European natives than French is, as 13.3% of Europe's population uses the language daily.

Reading and Pronunciation in the German

Ä, ä - ay

Ai - ie

Au - ow

Äu - oy

Ay – ie

B – p

C – ts *(before e,i,ä,ö,ts)*

Ch – kh *(read paragraph below)*

Ch – k *(before s)*

D – t *(end of word or between vowel and consonant)*

Eu – oy

G – g

G – if at the end of the word pronounced as "k" *(weg pronounced as vek)*

J – y

Ö ö - ooh

S – z

ß – ess *(like double "ss")*

Sch – sh

Tsch – ch

Tz – ts

Ü ü - uyuh

V – f

W – v

Z – ts

Ö – vr

Y – ew

The Program

I | I am - Ich | Ich bin
With you - Mit dir / mit euch
With him / with her - Mit ihm / mit ihr
With us - Mit uns
For you - Für dich / (**Plural**) für euch
Without him - Ohne ihn
Without them - Ohne sie
Always - Immer
Was - War
This - Das
Is - Ist
Sometimes - Manchmal
Today – Heute
You - Du, dich, dir, ihr, sie, *and* ihnen
You (plural) **-** Euch
Are you / you are - Bist Du, seid ihr, Sind Sie
Better - Lieber, besser
He - Er / sie /
She - es / it
From - Von

Are you at the house?
Bist du zu Hause?
I am always with her
Ich bin immer mit ihr
I am from Germany
Ich bin von Deutschland
Are you from Germany?
Sind Sie von Deutschland?
I am with you
Ich bin mit Dir, (pl.) euch
Are you alone today?
Bist du heute allein?
This is for you
Das ist für Dich (Pl.) euch
Sometimes I go without him.
Manchmal gehe ich ohne ihn.

I was - Ich war
To be - Zu sein
The - Der, die, das
Same - Gleich, selbe
Good - Gut
Here - Hier
It's / it is - Es ist
And - Und
Between - Zwischen
Now - Jetzt
Later / After - Später / nach
If - Wenn
Yes - Ja
Then - Dann
Tomorrow - Morgen
Also / too / as well - Auch

I was home at 5pm
Ich war um 17 Uhr zu Hause
Between now and tomorrow.
Zwischen jetzt und morgen.
It's better to be home later.
Es ist besser, später zu Hause zu sein.
If this is good, then I am happy.
Wenn es gut ist, dann bin ich glücklich.
Yes, you are very good
Ja, Sie sind sehr gut
I was here with them
Ich war hier mit ihnen
The same day
Der selbe Tag

*In the German language the masculine form of the article "the" is *der*, the feminine form is *die*, and the neuter form is *das*. It's sometimes hard to decipher whether a noun is masculine or feminine in the German language, so most people who study this language memorize the article as they go along. The article of all German nouns in the plural form automatically becomes *die*.

*In German, adjectives precede the noun. All nouns begin with capital letters, and verbs are lowercase letters.

Maybe - Vielleicht
Even if - Sogar wenn
Afterwards - Nachher
Worse - Schlechter
Where - Wo
Everything - Alles
Somewhere - Irgendwo
What - Was?
Almost - Fast
There - Da, dort
Okay - Okay

Even if I go now
Sogar wenn ich jetzt gehe
Where is everything?
Wo ist alles?
Maybe somewhere
Vielleicht irgend wo
What? I am almost there
Was? Ich bin fast da
Where are you?
Sie sind wo? / Du bist wo?
You and I
Sie, Du und ich
This is for us.
Das ist für uns.

*In the German language, *da* means "there," while *dort* means "over there."
*In German, "you" could either translate *du, dich, dir, ihr, euch, sie,* or *ihnen*.
Du is the nominative informal "you" (*sie* is the formal), *dich* is the accusative "you" (formal: *sie*), and *dir* is the dative "you" (formal: *ihnen*).
Nominative simply means "you." "You are German?" / *Du bist Deutsch?*
Accusative is the direct object: "I see you" / *ich sehe dich* or "I love you" / *ich liebe dich.*
Dative is the indirect object in the sentence (from someone / to someone / for someone):
- "I must give you" / *ich muss dir geben*
- "I want to show you" / *Ich möchte dir zeigen*
Plural "you"
- nominative informal *ihr* (formal: *sie*) / accusative informal *euch* (formal: *sie*)
Dative is *euch* (formal: *ihnen*).

House / home - Haus / zuhause
In / at - In
Car - Auto
Already - Schon
Good morning - Guten Morgen
How are you? - Wie geht es Ihnen, Dir
Where are you from? - Woher Sind Sie, bist Du
Me - Mir / mich
Hello - Hallo / Guten Tag
What is your name? - Was ist Dein Name?
How old are you? - Wie alt sind Sie, bist Du
Son - Sohn
Daughter - Tochter
Your - (*inf*) Deinem, dein, deine / (*form*) Ihr, ihre
Very - Sehr
Hard – Hart
Hard (as in difficult) - Schwierig
Still - Noch

She is not in the car, so maybe she is still at the house?
Sie ist ohne Auto, vielleicht ist sie noch im Haus
I am already in the car with your son and daughter
Ich bin schon im Auto mit Deinem Sohn und Tochter
Good morning, how are you today?
Guten Morgen, Wie geht es Ihnen, Dir, heute?
Hello, what is your name?
Guten Tag, was ist Ihr, Dein, Name?
How old are you?
Wie alt sind Sie, bist Du
This is very hard, but it's not impossible
Das ist sehr schwer, aber nicht unmöglich
Where are you from?
Von wo sind Sie, bist Du?

*The definition of *woher* is "from where."

*In German the pronoun "me" could either be translated *mich* or *mir*. *Mich* is an accusative direct pronoun, for example, "you like me?" / *du magst mich?* while *mir* is the dative indirect object, from somebody / to somebody / for somebody, for example, "give me" / *gib mir*.

Thank you - Danke Ihnen, Dir
For - Für
This is - Das ist
Time - Zeit
But / however - Aber
No / not - Nein / nicht
I am not - Ich bin nicht
Away - Weit, weg
That - Das, Dass
Similar - Ähnlich
Other / Another - Anderer, ein anderer
Side - Seite
Until - Bis
Yesterday - Gestern
Without us - Ohne uns
Since - Seit
Day - Tag
Before - Vorher / vor dem
With - Mit
Night - Nacht
Without you - Ohne Sie, Dich
I want - Ich will, möchte

I need to be there at night
Ich muss dort sein bei Nacht
Thank you, Kenneth.
Danke, Kenneth.
It's almost time
Es ist fast Zeit
I am not here, I am far away
Ich bin nicht hier, ich bin weg
That house is similar to ours.
Das ist ein ähnliches Haus
I am from the other side
Ich bin von der anderen Seite
But I was here until late yesterday
Aber ich war hier bis spät gestern
Since the other day
Seit dem anderen Tag

I say / I am saying - Ich sage, Ich bin dabei zu sagen
What time is it? - Welche Zeit ist es, wie spät ist es
Everywhere /wherever - Überall, wo auch immer
I go / I am going - Ich gehe
My - Mein, meiner, meins
Cousin - **(M)** Kusin, **(F)** Kusine
I need / I must - Ich brauche / Ich muss
Right now - Genau jetzt
To see – Zu sehen
Light - Licht
Outside - Draußen
That is - Das ist
I see / I am seeing - Ich sehe

I am saying no / I say no
Ich sage nein
I want to see this during the day
Ich will das am Tag sehen
I see this everywhere
Ich sehe das überall
I am happy without any of my cousins here
Ich bin glücklich ohne meine Kusinen hier
You need to be at home.
Du solltest zu Hause sein.
I see light outside
Ich sehe Licht draußen
What time is it right now?
Wie spät ist es genau jetzt?

*In German *am* could be translated "in the," "on the," "at the," or "during."

*A very important rule in German: whenever a conjugated verb is the first part of the sentence, it stays the same as its English counterpart. But in case the conjugated verb isn't the first part of the sentence, it will usually be placed at the end: "because I want this car" / *weil dieses Auto möchte*. Whenever a sentence contains two verbs, the second verb will usually appear at the end of the sentence (unlike in English in which the infinitive always follows the conjugated verb): "I want to see this in the day" / *Ich will das am Tag sehen*. There are exceptions, though. For example, the verb "to know" / *wissen* isn't moved to the end of the sentence in this case: "I must know where is the house" / *Ich muss wissen wo das Haus ist*.

To be - Sein
Place - Platz
Easy - Leicht
To find - Zu finden
To wait - Zu warten
To sell - Zu verkaufen
To use - Zu gebrauchen
To know - Zu wissen
To decide - Zu entscheiden
Between - Zwischen

This place is easy to find
Dieser Platz ist leicht zu finden
I am saying to wait until tomorrow
Ich sage bis morgen zu warten
It's easy to sell this table
Es ist leicht diesen Tisch zu verkaufen
I want to use this
Ich möchte das gebrauchen
Where is the book?
Wo ist das Buch?
I need to decide myself between both places
Ich muss mich entscheiden zwischen den beiden Plätzen
I need to know that everything is ok
Ich muss wissen dass alles ok ist

*In German, the article "this" preceding a noun is *dieser, diese, dieses,* or *dies*. *Dieser* is masculine nominative, feminine nominative is *diese*, and neutral nominative is *dieses* or *dies*.

*In German the preposition "to" has several definitions. *Nach* is used to indicate movement and going to a country or a geographical location. *Auf* is "to attend or be on top of something": *Ich gehe auf die Straße* / "I go to the street." *Zu* is "to a place" or corresponding to a verb. *In* is "to go inside a place." *An* is used to indicate "to a precise spot or vicinity." *Beim* means "to the"; *nahe beim* means "next to the," "close to the," or "near the." **Note:** Don't stress yourself with these prepositions, since many Germans don't even know the difference between them.

*"I need" / *ich brauche* and "I must" / *Ich muss* is used interchangeably throughout this program when translating "I need."

A - Ein, eine
Because - Weil
To buy - Zu kaufen
Both - Beide
Them / they / Their - Ihnen / sie / deren, Ihr
Each / Every - Jeden, jeder
To understand - Zu verstehen
Problem / Problems – Problem / probleme
I do / I am doing - Ich mache
To look - Zu Sehen / zu schauen
Myself - Ich, mich, selber
Enough - Genug
Food - Essen
Water - Wasser
Hotel - Hotel

I like this hotel because it's near the beach
Ich mag dieses Hotel, weil es in der Nähe des Strandes ist
I want to look at the view.
Ich möchte mir die Aussicht ansehen.
I want to buy a bottle of water
Ich möchte eine Flasche Wasser kaufen
Do it like this!
Mach es so!
Both of them have enough food
Beide haben genug zu essen
I need to understand the problem
Ich muss das Problem verstehen
I have a view of the city from the hotel.
Vom Hotel habe ich einen Blick auf die Stadt
I do what I want.
Ich tue, was ich will.

*The German grammatical rule concerning moving the second and third verb(s) to the end applies in most sentences unless the sentence is broken in parts, separated either by a comma or an "and."

To - Zu, an, auf, bis, in, nach, beim
I like - Ich mag / Ich liebe
There is / There are - Da ist / es sind
Family / Parents - Familie, Eltern
Why - Warum
To say - Zu sagen
Something - Etwas
To go - Zu gehen
Ready - Fertig
Soon - Bald
To work - Zu arbeiten
Who - Wer
Important - Wichtig

I like to be at home with my parents
Ich liebe es zuhause mit meinen Eltern zu sein
Why do I need to say something important?
Warum muss ich etwas Wichtiges sagen?
I am there with him
Ich bin dort mit ihm
I am busy, but I need to be ready soon
Ich bin beschäftigt, aber ich muss bald fertig sein
I like to work
Ich mag arbeiten
Who is there?
Wer ist dort?
I want to know if they are here.
Ich will wissen, ob sie hier sind.
I can go outside.
Ich kann nach draußen gehen.
There are seven dolls
Es sind sieben Puppen

*In German, if three verbs exist in the same sentence (Verb A, B, and C), Verb A is placed at the beginning of the sentence (as its English counterpart), while Verbs B and C are placed at the end and are inverted. So the chronological order is A, C, B. Take a look at the second sentence of this page (keep in mind that "to know" / *wissen* is an exception). Notice: "to say" / *sagen* and "I have" / *habe* are inverted.

How much - Wieviel(e)
To take - Zu nehmen
With me - Mit mir
Instead - Anstatt
Only - Nur
When - Wann
I can / Can I? - Ich kann
Or - Oder
Were - Waren
Without me - Ohne mich
Fast - Schnell
Slow - Langsam
Cold - Kalt
Inside - Drinnen
To eat - Zu essen
Hot - Heiß / warm
To Drive - Zu fahren

How much money do I need to bring with me?
Wieviel Geld brauche ich mitzunehmen?
I like to eat bread instead of rice.
Ich esse gerne Brot statt Reis.
Only when you can
Nur wann Du kannst
Go there without me.
Geh ohne mich dorthin.
I need to drive the car very fast or very slowly
Ich muss das Auto sehr schnell oder sehr langsam fahren
It is cold in the library
Es ist kalt in der Bibliothek
I like to eat a hot meal for my lunch.
Ja, Ich liebe das warm zum Mittagessen essen

*This *isn't* a phrase book! The purpose of this book is *solely* to provide you with the tools to create *your own* sentences!

*In German, whenever asking a question, the pronoun follows the conjugated verb. As you can see in the first sentence: "how much money do I need to take?" / *Wieviel Geld brauche **ich** mitzunehmen?* The pronoun *ich* / "I" follows the conjugated verb *brauche* / "I need."

To answer - Zu antworten
To fly - Zu fliegen
Today - Heute
To travel - Zu reisen
To learn - Zu lernen
To swim - Zu schwimmen
To practice - Zu üben
To play - Zu spielen
To leave - Zu lassen
To look for / to search - Zu suchen
I go to - Ich gehe zu
How - Wie
Near / Close - Nahe, nah
Many /much /a lot - Viele / viel
First – Erst / erstens
Time / Times - Zeit, Mal

I need to answer many questions
Ich muss viele Fragen beantworten
I want to fly today
Ich will heute fliegen
I need to learn to swim
Ich muss shwimmen lernen
I want to learn how to play better tennis.
Ich möchte lernen, wie man besser Tennis spielt.
Everything is about the money.
Alles dreht sich ums Geld.
I want to leave my dog at home.
Ich möchte meinen Hund zu Hause lassen.
I want to travel the world.
Ich möchte die Welt bereisen.
Since the first time
Seit dem ersten Mal
The children are yours
Die Kinder sind Deine

*With the knowledge you've gained so far, now try to create your own sentences!

Nobody / anyone - Niemand, irgend einer
Against - Gegen
Us - Uns
To visit - Zu besuchen
Mom / Mother - Mama/ Mutter
To give - Zu geben
Which - Welcher
To meet - Zu treffen
Someone - Jemand
Just - Genau
To walk - Zu gehen
Around - Um
Towards - Gegen
Than - Als
Nothing / Anything - Nichts

Something is better than nothing
Etwas ist besser als (gar) nichts
I am against him
Ich bin gegen ihn
We go to visit my family each week.
Wir gehen jede Woche meine Familie besuchen
I need to give you something
Ich muss Dir etwas geben
Do you want to meet someone?
Wollen Sie jemanden treffen?
I am here on Wednesdays as well.
Ich bin hier auch am Mittwoch
You do this everyday?
Sie machen das jeden Tag?
You need to walk around the school.
Sie müssen um die Schule herumgehen.
Is it possible to look for this book in the library.
Kann man dieses Buch in der Bibliothek suchen?
Is this place near?
Ist dieser Ort in der Nähe?

I have - Ich habe
Don't - Nicht
Friend - Freund
To borrow - Zu borgen
To look like - Aussehen wie/ ähneln
Grandfather - Großvater
To want – Zu möchten
To stay - Zu bleiben
To continue – Weiter machen / fortsetzen
Book - Buch
Mine - Mein
Way - Straße/ Weg
That's why - Darum
To show - Zu zeigen
To prepare - Vorbereiten
I am not going - Ich gehe nicht

Do you want to look like Arnold
Wollen Sie aussehen wie Arnold?
I want to borrow this book for my grandfather
Ich möchte das Buch für meinen Großvater ausborgen
I want to stay in Munich because I have a friend there.
Ich habe einen Freund, darum möchte ich in München bleiben
I don't want to see anyone here
Ich möchte niemanden hier sehen
I need to show you how to prepare breakfast
Ich möchte Dir zeigen wie man Früstück macht
Why don't you have the book?
Warum haben Sie das Buch nicht?
That is incorrect, I don't need the car today
Das stimmt nicht, Ich brauche nicht das Auto heute
That book is mine
Dieses Buch gehört mir

*In German, "don't" comes after the verb: "I don't need" / *ich brauche nicht*.

*In German, you would say "to **make** breakfast" and not "to prepare breakfast."

To remember – Zu merken
German - Deutsch
Number - Nummer
Hour - Stunde
Dark / darkness - Dunkel Dunkelheit
About - Über, ungefähr
Grandmother - Großmutter
Five - Fünf
Minute / minutes - Minute / Minuten
More - Mehr
To think - Zu denken
To do - Machen
To come - Zu kommen
To hear - Zu Hören
Last - Letzte(r)
To talk / to speak - Zu sprechen

I want to learn how to speak perfect German.
Ich möchte perfekt Deutsch sprechen lernen

I need to remember your number
Ich muss deine Telefonnummer merken

This is the last hour of darkness
Dies ist die letzte Stunde der Dunkelheit

I want to come with you.
Ich möchte mit dir kommen.

I can hear my grandmother speaking German.
Ich kann meine Großmutter Deutsch sprechen hören.

I need to think about this more.
Darüber muss ich noch nachdenken.

From here to there, it's only five minutes
Von hier nach dort, sind es nur fünf Minuten

I can work today
Ich kann heute arbeiten

*This *isn't* a phrase book! The purpose of this book is *solely* to provide you with the tools to create *your own* sentences!

To leave - Weggehen
Again - Nochmals, wieder
Early - Früh
Germany - Deutschland
To bring - Zu bringen
To try - Zu versuchen
To rent - Zu mieten
Without her - Ohne sie
We are - Wir sind
To turn off - Ausschalten
To ask – Zu bitten
To stop - Zu stoppen
Permission - Erlaubnis
Goodbye - Auf Wiedersehen
Tonight - Heute Nacht

Goodbye, my friend.
Auf Wiedersehen, mein Freund.

He must go and rent a house at the beach.
Er muss weggehen und ein Haus am Strand mieten

We are here for a long time
Wir sind hier für eine lange Zeit

I need to turn off the lights early tonight
Ich muss Das Licht heute Nacht früh ausmachen

We want to stop here
Wir wollen hier anhalten

We are from Frankfurt
Wir sind aus Frankfurt

Your doctor is in the same building.
Dein Arzt ist im selben Gebäude.

In order to leave you have to ask permission.
Um zu gehen, musst du um Erlaubnis fragen.

*The definition of *am* is "at the," "on the," "by the," or "to the."
*In German, the definition of *um* is "for, about, at (time)."

*In German, the definition of *im* is "in the," "at the."

To open - Zu öffnen
To buy - Zu kaufen
To pay - Zu bezahlen
Last - Letzte
Without - Ohne
Sister - Schwester
To hope - Zu hoffen
To live – Zu wohnen, leben
Nice to meet you - Schön Sie zu treffen, Schön Sie kennen zu lernen
Name - Vorname
Last name - Nachname
To return – Zurück / kommen
Enough - Genug
Door - Tür

I need to open the door for my sister
Ich muss die Tür für meine schwester öffnen

I need to buy something
Ich muss etwas kaufen

I want to meet your brothers.
Ich möchte deine Brüder treffen.

Nice to meet you, what is your name and your last name?
Schön Sie zu treffen, was ist ihre Vorname und ihre Nachname?

We can hope for a better future.
Wir können auf eine bessere Zukunft hoffen.

It is impossible to live without problems.
Es ist unmöglich, ohne Probleme zu leben.

I want to return to the United States.
Ich möchte in die Vereinigten Staaten zurückkehren.

Why are you sad right now?
Warum bist Du traurig genau jetzt?

Our house is on the mountain.
Unser Haus liegt am Berg.

To happen - Zu geschehen
To order - Zu befehlen
To drink - Zu trinken
Excuse me - Verzeihung
Child - Kind
Woman - Frau
To begin / to start - Zu beginnen
To finish - Zu enden / beenden
To help - Zu helfen
To smoke - Zu rauchen
To love - Zu lieben

This needs to happen today.
Das muss heute geschehen
Excuse me, my child is here as well
Verzeihung, mein Kind ist auch hier
I want to order a soup.
Ich möchte eine Suppe bestellen.
We want to start the class soon.
Wir wollen bald mit dem Unterricht beginnen.
In order to finish at three o'clock this afternoon, I need to finish soon
Um heute Nachmittag um drei Uhr fertig zu sein, muss ich es bald fertig machen
I don't want to smoke again
Ich will nicht wieder rauchen
I want to help
Ich möchte helfen
I love you
Ich liebe Sie, dich
I see you
Ich sehe Sie, dich
I need you
Ich brauche Sie, dich

*"I don't want" is *ich will nicht*.

To read - Zu lesen
To write - Zu schreiben
To teach - Zu unterrichten
To close - Zu schließen
To turn on - Anmachen
To prefer - Vorziehen
To choose – Wählen
To put - Hinlegen
Less - Weniger
Sun - Sonne
Month - Monat
I talk - Ich rede, spreche
Exact - Genau
Sky - Himmel
Sun - Sonne
High - Hoch

I need this book to learn how to read and write in German.
Ich brauche dieses Buch, um Deutsch lesen und schreiben zu lernen
I want to teach English in Germany
Ich möchte in Deutschland Englisch unterrichten
I want turn on the lights and close the door.
Ich will das Licht anmachen und die Tür schließen.
I want to pay less than you.
Ich möchte weniger bezahlen als du.
I prefer to put this here.
Ich stelle das lieber hier her.
I speak with the boy and the girl in German.
Ich spreche mit dem Mädel und Jungen auf Deutsch.
There is sun outside today.
Ich sehe die Sonne heute
Is it possible to know the exact date?
Ist es möglich das genaue Datum zu wissen?
I want to go to sleep
Ich möchte schlafen gehen
Where is the airport?
Wo ist der Flughafen?
The sun is high in the sky.
Die Sonne steht hoch am Himmel.

To exchange - Eintauschen
To call - Zu rufen / Anrufen
Brother - Bruder
Dad - Vater
To sit - Zu sitzen
Together - Zusammen
To change - Zu ändern
Of course - Auf jeden Fall
Welcome - Willkommen
During - Während
Years - Jahre
Sky - Himmel
Up - Oben
Down - Unten
Sorry - Tut mir Leid
To follow - Nachgehen
Her - Sie, ihr
Big - Groß
New - Neu
Never – Niemals
His / hers – Sein / ihr
Far - Weit

I am never able to exchange this money at the bank.
Ich will niemals das Geld in der Bank eintauschen
I want to call my brother and my dad today
Ich will meinen Bruder und Vater heute anrufen
Of course I can come to the theater, and I want to sit together with you and with your sister
Auf jeden Fall kann ich zum Theater kommen und ich möchte mit Dir and Deiner Schwester zusammen sitzen
If you look under the table, you can see the new rug.
Wenn du unter den Tisch schaust, kannst du den neuen Teppich sehen.
I am sorry.
Es tut mir leid.
I can see the sky from the window.
Ich kann den Himmel vom Fenster aus sehen.
The dog wants to follow me to the store.
Der Hund will mir in den Laden folgen.

To allow - Zu Lassen
To believe - Zu glauben
Morning - Morgen
Except - Außer
To promise - Zu versprechen
Good night - Gute Nacht
To recognize - Zu erkennen
People - Leute
To move - Zu bewegen,
To move - Umziehen
Different - Verschieden
Different - Anderer
Man - Mann
To enter - Eintreten
To receive - Zu empfangen
Throughout - Durch und durch
Through - Durch
Him - Ihn, ihm
His - Sein

I need to allow him to go with us.
Ich muss ihm erlauben, mit uns zu gehen.
He is a different man now.
Er ist jetzt ein anderer Mann.
I believe everything except for this
Ich glaube alles, außer dem
Come here quickly.
Komm schnell her.
I can't recognize him.
Ich kann ihn nicht erkennen.
I need to put your cat to another chair
Ich muss deine Katze auf einen anderen Stuhl legen
I see the sun in the morning from the kitchen
Ich sehe die Sonne am Morgen aus der Küche
I go into the house from the front entrance and not through the yard.
Ich gehe durch den Vordereingang ins Haus und nicht durch den Hof.

To wish - Zu wünschen
Bad - Schlecht
To get - Zu bekommen
To forget - Zu vergessen
Everybody / Everyone - Jeder
Although - Trotzdem
To feel - Zu fühlen
Great - Groß
Next - Nächste
To like - Gerne haben
In front - Vor
Person - Person
Behind - Hinter
Well - Gut
Restaurant - Restaurant
Bathroom - Toilette

I don't want to wish anything bad
Ich will Dir nichts schlechtes wünschen
I must forget everybody from my past.
Ich muss alle aus meiner Vergangenheit vergessen.
To feel well I must take vitamins
Um mich wohl zu fühlen, muss ich Vitamine nehmen
I am close to the person behind you
Ich bin nah bei der Person hinter Ihnen
There is a great person in front of me
Da ist eine grosse Person vor mir
Which is the best restaurant in the area?
Welches ist das beste Restaurant in der Gegend?
I can feel the heat.
Ich kann die Hitze spüren.
I need to repair a part of the cabinet in the bathroom.
Ich muss etwas am Schrank im Badezimmer reparieren.
I want a car before the next year
Ich will ein Auto vor dem nächsten Jahr
I like the house, but it is very small.
Ich möchte das Haus gerne, aber es ist sehr klein

To remove - Wegnehmen, zu entfernen
Please - Bitte
Beautiful - Schön
To lift - Zu heben
Include / Including – Inbegriffen, einschließlich
Belong - Gehört dazu
To hold - Zu halten
To check – Zu prüfen
Small - Klein
Real - Wirklich, echt
Week - Woche
Size - Größe
Even though – Trotzdem, obwohl
Doesn't - Nicht
So - Also
Price Preis

She wants to remove this door, please
Sie möchte die Tür wegnehmen, bitte
This doesn't belong here, I need to check again
Das gehört hier nicht, Ich musst nochmal prüfen
This week the weather was very beautiful
Diese Woche das Wetter war sehr schön
Is that a real diamond?
Ist das ein echter Diamant?
We need to check the size of the house
Wir müssen die Größe das Haus nachprüfen
I want to lift this.
Ich möchte das hochheben.
Can you please put the wood in the fire?
Kannst du bitte das Holz ins Feuer legen?
Can you please hold my hand?
Kannst du bitte meine Hand halten?
I can pay this although the price is expensive
Ich kann das bezahlen obwohl der Preis hoch ist
Including everything is this price correct?
Mit allem, ist der Preis richtig?

*In German, its more grammatically correct to say "with everything" rather than "including everything," as you can see with the last sentence.

Building Bridges

In Building Bridges, we take six conjugated verbs that have been selected after studies I have conducted for several months in order to determine which verbs are most commonly conjugated, and which are then automatically followed by an infinitive verb. For example, once you know how to say, "I need," "I want," "I can," and "I like," you will be able to connect words and say almost anything you want more correctly and understandably. The following three pages contain these six conjugated verbs in first, second, third, fourth, and fifth person, as well as some sample sentences. Please master the entire program up until *here* prior to venturing onto this section.

I want - Ich möchte
I need - Ich brauche
I can - Ich kann
I like - Ich mag
I go - Ich gehe
I have - Ich habe
I must - Ich muss

I want to go to my apartment
Ich will zu meiner Wohnung gehen

I can go with you to the bus station
Ich kann mit Ihnen zur Bushaltestelle gehen

I need to walk outside the museum.
Ich brauche einen Spaziergang beim Museum.

I like to eat oranges.
Ich esse gerne Orangen.

I am going to teach a class
Ich gehe eine Klasse unterrichten

I have to speak to my teacher
Ich muss mit meinem Lehrer sprechen

Please master *every* single page up until here prior to attempting the following two pages!

You want / do you want
Du möchtest / möchtest Du?
He wants / does he want
Er möchte? / möchte er?
She wants / does she want
Sie möchte / möchte sie?
We want / do we want
Wir möchten / möchten wir?
They want / do they want
Sie möchten / möchten sie?
You (plural/ formal sing) want / do you want?
Sie möchten / möchten Sie?

You need / do you need
Du brauchst / brauchst Du?
He needs / does he need
Er braucht / braucht er?
She needs / does she need
Sie braucht / braucht sie?
We need / do we need
Wir brauchen / brauchen wir?
They need / do they need
Sie brauchen / brauchen sie?
You (plural/ formal sing) need / do you need?
Sie brauchen / brauchen Sie?

You can / can you
Du kannst / kannst Du?
He can / can he
Er kann / kann er?
She can / can she
Sie kann / kann sie?
We can / can we
Wir können / können wir?
They can / can they
Sie können / können sie?
You (plural/ formal sing) can / can you?
Sie können / können Sie?

You like / do you like
Du magst? / magst du?
He likes / does he like
Er mag / mag er?
She like / does she like
Sie mag / mag sie?
We like / do we like
Wir mögen / mögen wir?
They like / do they like
Sie mögen / mögen sie?
You (plural/ formal sing) like / do you like?
Sie mögen / mögen Sie?

You go / do you go
Du gehst / gehst Du?
He goes / does he go
Er geht / geht er?
She goes / does she go
Sie geht / geht sie?
We go / do we go
Wir gehen / gehen wir?
They go / do they go
Sie gehen / gehen sie?
You (plural/ formal sing) go / do you go?
Sie gehen / gehen Sie?

You have / do you have
Du hast / hast Du?
He has / does he have
Er hat / hat er ?
She has / does she have
Sie hat / hat sie?
We have / do we have
Wir haben / haben wir?
They have / do they have
Sie haben / haben sie?
You (plural/ formal sing) have / do you have?
Sie haben / haben Sie
Do you want to go?
Möchtest Du gehen?

Does he want to fly?
Möchte er fliegen?

We want to swim
Wir wollen schwimmen

Do they want to run?
Wollen sie rennen?

Do you need to clean?
Müssen Sie sauber machen?
Musst Du sauber machen?

She needs to sing a song
Sie muss ein Lied singen

We need to travel
Wir müssen reisen

They don't need to fight
Sie müssen nicht kämpfen

You (plural) need to save your money.
Ihr (Plural) müsst euer Geld sparen.

Can you hear me?
Kannst Du mich hören?

He can dance very well
Er kann sehr gut tanzen

We can go out tonight
Wir können heute abend ausgehen

The fireman can break the door during an emergency.
Der Feuerwehrmann kann im Notfall die Tür aufbrechen.

Do you like to eat here?
Essen Sie gerne hier
Isst Du gerne hier?

He likes to spend time here
Er mag hier Zeit verbringen

We like to fix the house
Wir lieben das Haus zu reparieren

They like to cook
Sie lieben zu kochen

You (plural) like to play soccer.
Ihr (Plural) spielt gerne Fußball.

Do you go to the movies on weekends?
Gehst du am Wochenende ins Kino?

He goes fishing
Er geht fischen

We are going to relax
Wir gehen uns ausruhen

They go out to eat at a restaurant every day.
Sie gehen jeden rausgehen und in einem Restaurant essen.

Do you have money?
Haben Sie Geld?
Hst Du Geld?

She must look outside
Sie muss nach draußen schauen

We have to sign our names
Wir müssen unsere Namen unterschreiben

They have to send the letter
Sie müssen den Brief abschicken

You (plural) have to stand in line.
Ihr (Plural) müsst in der Schlange stehen.

Days of the Week
Sunday - Sonntag
Monday - Montag
Tuesday - Dienstag
Wednesday - Mittwoch
Thursday - Donnerstag
Friday - Freitag
Saturday - Samstag

Seasons
Spring - Frühling
Summer - Sommer
Autumn - Herbst
Winter - Winter

Cardinal Directions
North - Nord / **South** - Süd
East - Ost / **West** - West

Colors
Black - Schwarz
White - Weiss
Gray - Grau
Red - Rot
Blue - Blau
Yellow - Gelb
Green - Grün
Orange - Orange
Purple – Lila, Violett
Brown - Braun

Numbers
One - Eins
Two - Zwei
Three - Drei
Four - Vier
Five - Fünf
Six - Sechs
Seven - Sieben
Eight - Acht
Nine - Neun
Ten - Zehn

Conversational Dutch Quick and Easy
The Most Innovative Technique to Learn the Dutch Language

YATIR NITZANY

The Dutch Language

Dutch is not only the national language of the Netherlands but is also a national language of Belgium, and Suriname and the Dutch Antilles in South America. In Belgium, it's the official language of Flanders, the Northern region of the country, and is also spoken in Brussels by a minority. In Suriname and the Dutch Antilles, Dutch is still an official language but alongside several other languages.

Worldwide, there are over 23 million native speakers of Dutch. It is a popular second language in Germany and the north of France, and it's a growing language in Eastern Europe.

Dutch and English are languages that come from the same old Germanic root and Dutch is the third most popular Germanic language after English and German. Dutch vocabulary is mostly Germanic and incorporates more loan words from Romance languages than German but fewer than English.

In both Belgium and the Netherlands, the native official name for Dutch is *Nederlands*, and its dialects have their own names, e.g. Hollands ("Hollandic"), West-Vlaams ("West Flemish"), and Brabants ("Brabantian").

The word Dutch was derived from the Old Germanic word *theudisk*, one of the first names ever used for the non-Romance languages of Western Europe. It literally means "the language of the common people," that is, the native Germanic language. The term was used in opposition to Latin, which was the non-native language of writing and of the Catholic Church.

Reading and Pronunciation in Dutch

Vowels can be pronounced long or short, depending on whether they are followed by no, one, or two consonants. Diphthongs existing of two of the same vowels are pronounced in the same way as if a single one would be followed by no or one consonant.

a (short) – "ah" as in father
a (long) and *aa* – "ah" as in father but longer
e (short) – "eh" as in men
e (long) and *ee* – as the "a" in maze
i – as the "i" in bit
o (short) – "oh" as in of
o (long) and *oo* – "oh" as in boat
u (short) – "uh" as in buzz
u (long) and *uu* – "ew," but pronouncing the "e" a bit longer and the "w" a bit shorter. This sound is not found in English.

Diphthongs

eu – This sound is not found in English, but is pronounced as 'eux' in the French word 'deux'

oe – "ooh" as in pool
ui – combination of *a* and *uu*
au/ou – as in house
ei/ij – as the "igh" in light and high

j – like the "y" in you

ch/g – a hard sound not found in English. It's a bit like the "J" in the Spanish name Juan. The best way to describe *ch* or *kh* is to say "ka" or "ha" while at the same time putting your tongue at the back of your throat and blowing air. It's pronounced similarly to the sound that you make while clearing your throat of phlegm.

*Please remember this whenever you come across any word containing a *ch* in this program.

I / I am - Ik / Ik ben
With you – Met jou / (**Plural**) met jullie
With him - Met hem / **with her** – met haar
With us – Met ons
For you – Voor jou / (**Plural**) voor jullie
Without him – Zonder hem
Without them – Zonder hen
Sometimes - Soms
Today - Vandaag
Are you / you are – Ben je, Zijn jullie
Better - Beter
You - Jij, je, jou / **You plural** - Jullie
He / he is - Hij / hij is
She / she is – Zij / zij is
From – Van / uit
This - Dit
Is - Is

Are you at the house?
Ben je thuis?
I am always with her.
Ik ben altijd met haar.
I am from the Netherlands.
Ik kom uit Nederland.
Are you from the Netherlands?
Kom je uit Nederland?
I am with you.
Ik ben met jou, (pl.) jullie.
Are you alone today?
Ben je alleen vandaag?
This is for you.
Dit is voor jou (Pl.) jullie.
Sometimes I go without him.
Soms ga ik zonder hem.

*"I am from …" can only be translated as "I come from…" The verb "to be" cannot be used in this sentence.

*In Dutch, in the event that a sentence begins with an adverb, the subject and verb change positions in the sentence.

Was - Was
I was – Ik was
To be - Zijn
The – De, het
Same – Zelfde, hetzelfde, dezelfde, gelijk
Good - Goed
Here - Hier
It's / it is – Het is
And - En
Between - Tussen
Now - Nu
Later / After - Later / Na
If - Als
Yes - Ja
Then - Dan
Tomorrow - Morgen
Okay – Oké
Also / too / as well - Ook

I was home at 5pm
Om 17.00 uur was ik thuis
Between now and tomorrow.
Tussen nu en morgen.
It's better to be home later.
Het is beter om later thuis te zijn.
If this is good, then I am happy.
Als dit goed is, ben ik blij.
Yes, you are very good
Ja, je bent erg goed
I was here with them
Ik was hier met hen
The same day
Dezelfde dag
You and I
Jij en ik

*In the Dutch language the masculine form of the article "the" is *de*, the feminine form is also *de*, and the neuter form is *het*. It's sometimes hard to decipher whether a noun is masculine or feminine in the Dutch language, so most people who study this language memorize the article as they go along.

Maybe - Misschien
You – Jij, je, jou
Even if – Zelfs als
Afterwards – Na, achteraf, nadien
Worse - Slechter
Where - Waar / **Somewhere** - Ergens
Everything - Alles
What - Wat
Almost - Bijna
There – Daar, er

Even if I go now
Zelfs als ik nu ga
Where is everything?
Waar is alles?
Maybe somewhere
Misschien ergens
What? I am almost there
Wat? Ik ben er bijna
Where are you?
Waar ben je?
This is for us.
Dit is voor ons.

*In the Dutch language, *daar* means "there," while *er* means "over there."
*In Dutch, "you" could either translate *je, jij, jou, u (formal)*
Je/jij is the nominative informal "you" (*u* is the formal), *je/jou* is the accusative "you" (formal: *u*), and je/*jou* is the dative "you" (formal: *u*).
Nominative simply means "you." "You are Dutch?" / *je/jij bent Nederlands?*
Accusative is the direct object: "I see you" / *ik zie je/jou* or "I love you" / *ik hou van je/jou*.
Dative is the indirect object in the sentence (from someone / to someone / for someone):
- "I must give you" / *ik moet je/jou geven*
- "I want to show you" / *ik wil je/jou laten zien*
Plural "you"
- Nominative: *jullie* / Accusative: *jullie* / Dative is *jullie*
The formal version of *u* is normally only used in formal organizations for people of a higher rank and in daily conversations for people who are older than you. E.g. some children will use the formal version for their grandparents; other children won't. But for strangers, the formal version is used.

House / home - Huis / thuis
In / at – In / bij
Car - Auto
Already - Al
Good morning - Goedemorgen
How are you? – Hoe gaat het met je/jou?
Where are you from? – Waar kom je vandaan?
Me - Me / mij
Hello - Hallo
What is your name? – Wat is je/jouw naam?
How old are you? – Hoe oud ben je/jij?
Son - Zoon / **Daughter** - Dochter
Your - *(form)* Uw / *(inf)* jouw
Very - Erg
Hard - Moeilijk
Still – Nog, nog steeds
So *(as in then)* – Dus

She doesn't have a car, so maybe she is still at the house?
Zij heeft geen auto, dus misschien is zij nog bij het huis?
I am already in the car with your son and daughter
Ik ben al in de auto met jouw zoon en dochter
Good morning, how are you today?
Goedemorgen, hoe gaat het met je vandaag?
Hello, what is your name?
Hallo, wat is je/jouw naam?
How old are you?
Hoe oud ben je/jij?
This is very hard, but it's not impossible
Dit is erg moeilijk, maar het is niet onmogelijk
Where are you from?
Waar kom je vandaan?

*"He is" is *hij is* / "she is" is *zij is*; however, in questions, the verb and subject change position; "she is?" *is zij?* / "he is?" *is hij?*

Waar... vandaan means "from where." The word *van* has many meanings, one of which is "from," but it cannot be used like this (*van*) in this sentence. It is a fixed expression and you have to use *vandaan* in this case.

* *Zij heeft geen auto* = "She has no car." "She is without a car" cannot be mirror translated into Dutch.

Thank you – Dank je
Thanks - Bedankt
For - Voor
A - Een
This is – Dit is
Time - Tijd
But / however – Maar, echter
No / not - Nee / niet
I am not – Ik ben niet
Away - Weg
That - Dat
Similar - Vergelijkbaar
Other / Another – Ander / andere
Side - Kant
Until – Tot, totdat
Yesterday - Gisteren
Without us – Zonder ons
Since - Sinds
Day - Dag
Before – Voor, voordat
With - Met

Thank you Kenneth.
Dank je, Kenneth.
It's almost time
Het is bijna tijd
I am not here, I am far away
Ik ben niet hier, ik ben weg
That house is similar to ours.
Dat is een vergelijkbaar huis
I am from the other side
Ik ben van de andere kant
But I was here until late yesterday
Maar ik was hier tot laat gisteren
Since the other day
Sinds de andere dag

*This *isn't* a phrase book! The purpose of this book is *solely* to provide you with the tools to create *your own* sentences!

What time is it? – Wat is de tijd? / hoe laat is het?
I want – Ik wil
Without you – Zonder jou
I go / I am going – Ik ga
My - Mijn
Cousin - (**Male**) Neef, (**Female**) Nicht
I need / I must – Ik heb … nodig / Ik moet
Right now – Direct, nu
Night - Nacht
To see - Zien
Light - Licht
Outside - Buiten
That is – Dat is
To be - Zijn

I want to see this during the day
Ik wil dit tijdens de dag zien
I am happy without any of my cousins here
Ik ben blij zonder mijn (M)neven/(F)nichten hier
I need to be there at night
Ik moet daar 's nachts zijn
You need to be at home.
Je moet thuis zijn.
I see light outside
Ik zie licht buiten
What time is it right now?
Hoe laat is het nu? / Wat is de tijd nu?

*A very important rule in Dutch: whenever a conjugated verb is the first part of the sentence, it stays the same as its English counterpart. But in case the conjugated verb isn't the first part of the sentence, it will usually be placed at the end: "because I want this car" / *omdat ik deze auto wil*. Whenever a sentence contains two verbs, the second verb will usually appear at the end of the sentence (unlike in English in which the infinitive always follows the conjugated verb): "I want to see this in the day" / *Ik wil dit overdag zien*. There are exceptions, though. For example, the verb "to know" / *weten* isn't moved to the end of the sentence in this case: "I must know where is the house" / *Ik moet weten waar het huis is*.

*In Dutch, 's is a fixed expression: "At night" - *'s nachts* / "In the morning" - *'s morgens* / "In the afternoon" - *'s middags*

Place - Plaats
Easy - Makkelijk
To find – Vinden
To look for / to search – Zoeken
Near, close – Dichtbij / **Next to** - Naast
To wait – Wachten
To sell – Verkopen
To use – Gebruiken
To know – Weten
To decide – Beslissen
Between - Tussen
To – Te, naar
That (conjunction) – Dat

This place is easy to find
Deze plaats is makkelijk te vinden
I am saying to wait until tomorrow
Ik zeg te wachten tot morgen
It's easy to sell this table
Het is makkelijk om deze tafel te verkopen
I want to use this
Ik wil dit gebruiken
Where is the book?
Waar is het boek?
I need to decide between both places
Ik moet beslissen tussen beide plaatsen
I need to know that everything is ok
Ik moet weten dat alles oké is
Is it possible to look for this book in the library.
Kun je naar dit boek te zoeken in de bibliotheek?
Is this place near?
Is deze plek in de buurt?

*In Dutch, the article "this" preceding a noun is *dit, deze*. *Deze* is masculine nominative, feminine nominative is *deze*, and neutral nominative is *dit*.

*In Dutch, there are two forms for expressing "to," *naar* and *te*. *Naar* is "to" when talking about going to a specific place. E.g. "I am going to New York/the library/home." In combination with verbs, it is *te*.

*"I need" / *ik heb nodig* and "I must" / *Ik moet* is used interchangeably throughout this program when translating "I need."

Because - Omdat
To buy – Kopen
Both – Beide / allebei
Them / they / their - Hen / zij / hun
Each / Every - Elk, elke, ieder, iedere
Book - Boek
Mine - Mijn
To understand – Begrijpen
Problem / problems – Probleem / problemen
I do / I am doing – Ik doe
Of – Van, over
To look – Kijken
Myself - Mezelf
Enough - Genoeg
Food – Eten, voedsel / **Water** - Water
Hotel - Hotel

I like this hotel because it's near the beach
Dit hotel bevalt mij omdat het vlakbij het strand ligt.
I want to look at the view.
Ik wil naar het uitzicht kijken.
I want to buy a bottle of water
Ik wil een fles water kopen
Do it like this!
Doe het zo!
Both of them have enough food
Allebei hebben ze genoeg voedsel
That book is mine
Dat boek is van mij.
I have to understand the problem
Ik moet het problem begrijpen
I have a view of the city from the hotel.
Van het hotel heb ik uitzicht over de stad
I can work today
Ik kan vandaag werken
I do what I want.
Ik doe wat ik wil.

*The Dutch grammatical rule concerning moving the second and third verb(s) to the end applies in most sentences unless the sentence is broken in parts, separated either by a comma or an "and."

I like – Ik vind … leuk
There is / There are – Daar is, Er is / Daar zijn, Er zijn
Family / Parents – Familie / Ouders
Why - Waarom
To say – Zeggen
Something - Iets
To go – Gaan
Ready - Klaas
Soon – Snel, bijna
To work – Werken
Who - Wie
Important – Belangrijk, belangrijks

I like to be at home with my parents
Ik vind het leuk thuis te zijn met mijn ouders
Why do I need to say something important?
Waarom moet ik iets belangrijks zeggen?
I am there with him
Ik ben daar met hem
I am busy, but I have to be ready soon
Ik ben druk, maar ik moet bijna klaar zijn
I like to work
Ik vind het leuk te werken
Who is there?
Wie is daar?
I want to know if they are here.
Ik wil weten of ze hier zijn.
I can go outside.
Ik kan naar buiten gaan.
There are seven dolls
Er zijn zeven poppen

*In Dutch, if three verbs exist in the same sentence (Verb A, B, and C), Verb A is placed at the beginning of the sentence (as its English counterpart), while Verbs B and C are placed at the end and are inverted. So the chronological order is A, C, B. Take a look at the second sentence of this page (keep in mind that "to know" / *weten* is an exception).

*There is no verb for "like," so you have to translate it as "I find nice." You always have to put the object you like in between *vind* and *leuk*.

How much - Hoeveel
To take – Nemen
With me – Met mij
Instead – In plaats van
Only - Alleen
When - Wanneer
I can / can I? – Ik kan / Kan ik?
Or - Of
Were - Waren
Without me – Zonder mij
Fast - Snel
Slow - Langzaam
Cold - Koud
Inside - Binnen
To eat – Eten
Hot - Heet
To Drive – Rijden
I say / I am saying - Ik zeg

How much money do I need to bring with me?
Hoeveel geld moet ik meenemen?
I like to eat bread instead of rice.
Ik eet graag brood in plaats van rijst.
Only when you can
Alleen wanneer jij kan
Go there without me.
Ga daar zonder mij heen.
I need to drive the car very fast or very slowly
Ik moet doe auto erg snel of erg langzaam rijden
It is cold in the library
Het is koud in de bibliotheek
I like to eat a hot meal for my lunch.
Ja, ik vind het leuk dit warm te eten voor mijn lunch
I am saying no / I say no
Ik zeg nee

*In Dutch, whenever asking a question, the pronoun follows the conjugated verb. As you can see in the first sentence: "how much money do I need to take?" / *Hoeveel geld moet ik meenemen?* The pronoun *ik* / "I" follows the conjugated verb *moet* / "I need."

To answer – Antwoorden
To fly – Vliegen
Today - Vandaag
To travel – Reizen
To learn – Leren
How - Hoe
To swim – Zwemmen
To practice – Oefenen
To play – Spelen
To leave – Verlaten
Many / much / a lot – Veel
I go to – Ik ga naar
First – Eerst / eerste
Time / Times – Tijd / Tijden

I need to answer many questions
Ik moet veel vragen beantwoorden
I want to fly today
Ik wil vandaag vliegen
I need to learn to swim
Ik moet leren zwemmen
I want to learn how to play better tennis.
Ik wil graag beter leren tennissen.
Everything is about the money.
Alles draait om geld.
I want to leave my dog at home.
Ik wil mijn hond thuis laten.
I want to travel the world.
Ik wil de wereld rondreizen.
Since the first time
Sinds de eerste tijd
The children are yours
De kinderen zijn van jou

*In Dutch, *uw* is the formal and *jouw* is the informal; however, "yours" is *jou*. *Dit zijn jouw kinderen* = "These are your children," however, *de kinderen zijn van jou* = "The children are yours."

*With the knowledge you've gained so far, now try to create your own sentences!

Nobody / anyone - Niemand, iedereen
Against - Tegen
Us - Ons
To visit – Bezoeken
Mom / Mother - Mama/ Moeder
To give – Geven
Which – Welk, welke
To meet – Ontmoeten
Someone - Iemand
Just - Net
To walk – Wandelen
Around - Rond
Towards - Tegen
Than - Dan
Nothing – Niets
I see / I am seeing – Ik zie
Everywhere /wherever – Overal / waar dan ook

I see this everywhere
Ik zie dit overal
Something is better than nothing
Iets is beter dan niets
I am against him
Ik ben tegen hem
We go to visit my family each week.
We gaan elke week mijn familie bezoeken
I need to give you something
Ik moet je iets geven
Do you want to meet someone?
Wil je iemand ontmoeten?
I am here on Wednesdays as well.
Ik ben hier ook op woensdagen
You do this every day?
Je doet dit elke dag?
You need to walk around the school.
Je moet om de school lopen.
Where is the airport?
Waar is het vliegveld?

I have – Ik heb
Don't - Niet
Friend - Vriend
To borrow – Lenen
To look like – Eruit zien als
Grandfather – Opa, grootvader
To want – Willen
To stay – Blijven
To continue – Verder gaan
Way - Weg
That's why - Daarom
To show – Laten zien
To prepare - Voorbereiden
I am not going – Ik ga niet

Do you want to look like Arnold?
Wil je eruit zien als Arnold?

I want to borrow this book for my grandfather
Ik wil dit boek lenen voor mijn opa

I want to drive and to continue on this way to my house
Ik wil rijden en verder gaan op deze weg naar mijn huis

I want to stay in Utrecht because I have a friend there.
Ik heb een vriend, dat is waarom ik in Utrecht wil blijven

I don't want to see anyone here
Ik wil hier niemand zien

I need to show you how to prepare breakfast
Ik moet/wil je laten zien hoe ontbijt te maken

Why don't you have the book?
Waarom heb je het boek niet?

That is incorrect, I don't need the car today
Dat klopt niet, ik heb de auto niet nodig vandaag

*In Dutch, you would say "to **make** breakfast" and not "to prepare breakfast."

To remember – Onthouden
Dutch - Nederlands
Number - Nummer
Hour - Uur
Dark / darkness – Donker / Duisternis
About – Over, ongeveer
Grandmother – Oma, grootmoeder
Five - Vijf
Minute / minutes – Minuut / minuten
More - Meer
To think - Denken
To do – Doen
To come – Komen
To hear – Horen
Last – Laatst, laatste

I need to remember your number
Ik moet je/jouw nummer onthouden

This is the last hour of darkness
Dit is het laatste uur duisternis

I want to come with you.
Ik wil met je meegaan.

I can hear my grandmother speaking Dutch.
Ik hoor mijn oma Nederlands praten.

I need to think about this more.
Ik moet hier meer over nadenken.

From here to there, it's only five minutes
Van hier naar daar is het maar vijf minuten

*In Dutch, "your" – (formal) *Uw* / (informal) *jouw* – it is grammatically correct to use both, although Dutch people will have a strong preference for one of them depending on the sentence. This is something that cannot be explained; it is chosen based on a feeling.

To leave - Weggaan
Again – Nog een keer, nogmaals
The Netherlands - Nederland
To bring - Brengen
To try – Proberen
To rent – Huren
Without her – Zonder haar
We are – We zijn
To turn off - Uitzetten
To ask – Vragen
To stop – Stoppen
Permission - Toestemming

He needs to leave and rent a house at the beach
Hij moet weggaan en een huis bij het strand huren

We are here for a long time
We zijn hier voor lange tijd

I need to turn off the lights early tonight
Ik moet het licht vroeg uitdoen vandaag

We want to stop here
We willen hier stoppen

We are from Rotterdam.
Wij komen uit Rotterdam.

Your doctor is in the same building.
Uw arts is in hetzelfde gebouw.

In order to leave you have to ask permission.
Je moet toestemming vragen om te vertrekken.

I want to go to sleep
Ik wil gaan slapen.

*In Dutch, Om is a part of fixed expressions.
- "Ask for permission" = *vragen om toestemming*
- "Permission to" = *toestemming om te*

To open – Openen
To buy – Kopen
To pay – Betalen
Last – Laatst, laatste
Without - Zonder
Sister - Zus
To hope – Hopen
To live – Wonen, leven
Nice to meet you – Leuk je te leren kennen
Name - Voornaam
Last name - Achternaam
To return - Terugkomen
Enough - Genoeg
Door - Deur

I need to open the door for my sister
Ik moet de deur openen voor mijn zus
I need to buy something
Ik moet iets kopen
I want to meet your brothers.
Ik wil je broers ontmoeten.
Nice to meet you, what is your name and your last name?
Leuk je te leren kennen, wat je is voornaam en je achternaam?
We can hope for a better future.
We kunnen hopen op een betere toekomst.
It is impossible to live without problems.
Het is onmogelijk om zonder problemen te leven.
I want to return to the United States.
Ik wil terug naar de Verenigde Staten.
Why are you sad right now?
Waarom ben je verdrietig nu?

*In Dutch, "your" is *jouw*, however, in the case on this page, *je* is not the subject of the sentence, but the possessive determiner. In this sentence, it is interchangeable with *jouw*.

*In Dutch, *op* is a fixed expression: "To hope for" = *Hopen op*.

*This *isn't* a phrase book! The purpose of this book is *solely* to provide you with the tools to create *your own* sentences!

To happen – Gebeuren
To order – Bestellen
To drink – Drinken
Excuse me – Excuseer mij
Child - Kind
Woman - Vrouw
To begin / to start - Beginnen
To finish – Eindigen
To help – Helpen
To smoke – Roken
To love – Houden van
To talk / to speak – Praten / spreken

This needs to happen today
Dit moet gebeuren vandaag
Excuse me, my child is here as well
Excuseer mij, mijn kind is hier ook
I want to order a soup.
Ik wil graag een soep bestellen.
We want to start the class soon.
We willen spoedig met de les beginnen.
In order to finish at three o'clock this afternoon, I need to finish soon
Om vanmiddag om drie uur klaar te zijn, moet ik het snel afronden.
I want to learn how to speak perfect Dutch.
Ik wil perfect Nederlands leren spreken.
I don't want to smoke again
Ik wil niet weer roken
I want to help
Ik wil helpen
I love you
Ik hou van je/jou
I see you
Ik zie je/jou
I need you
Ik heb je/jou nodig

*"I don't want" is *ik wil niet*.

To read – Lezen
To write – Schrijven
To teach – Leren, les geven
To close – Sluiten
To turn on - Aanzetten
To prefer - Verkiezen
To choose - Kiezen
To put - Neerleggen
Less - Minder
Sun - Zon
Month - Maand
I talk – Ik spreek
Exact – Precies, exact(e)

I need this book to learn how to read and write in Dutch.
Ik heb dit boek nodig om Nederlands te leren lezen en schrijven.

I want to teach English in Holland.
Ik wil Engels lesgeven in Nederland.

I want turn on the lights and close the door.
Ik wil de lichten aandoen en de deur sluiten.

I want to pay less than you.
Ik wil minder betalen dan jij.

I prefer to put this here.
Ik plaats dit liever hier.

I speak with the boy and the girl in Dutch.
Ik spreek met de jongen en het meisje in het Nederlands.

There is sun outside today.
Vandaag is er buiten zon.

Is it possible to know the exact date?
Is het mogelijk de exacte datum te weten?

*With the knowledge you've gained so far, now try to create your own sentences!

To exchange – Ruilen, wisselen
To call – Bellen
Brother - Broer
Dad - Vader
To sit – Zitten
Together - Samen
To change – Veranderen
Of course - Natuurlijk
Welcome - Welkom
During - Tijdens
Years - Jaren
Sky - Hemel
Up - Boven
Down - Onder
Sorry - Sorry
To follow – Volgen
Her – Haar
Big - Groot
New - Nieuw
Never – Nooit
His / hers – Zijn / haar

I am never able to exchange this money at the bank.
Ik wil dit geld nooit wisselen bij de bank.

I want to call my brother and my dad today.
Ik wil mijn broer en mijn vader bellen vandaag.

Of course I can come to the theater, and I want to sit together with you and with your sister.
Natuurlijk kan ik naar het theater komen en ik wil samen met jou en je zus zitten.

If you look under the table, you can see the new rug.
Als je onder de tafel kijkt, zie je het nieuwe vloerkleed.

I am sorry.
Het spijt me.

The dog wants to follow me to the store.
De hond wil mij volgen naar de winkel.

To allow - Toestaan
To believe – Geloven
Morning - Morgen
Except - Behalve
To promise – Beloven
Good night - Goedenacht
To recognize – Herkennen
People - Mensen
To move – Bewegen, verhuizen
To sleep – Slapen
Far - Ver
Different – Verschillend, anders
Man - Man
To enter – Binnen komen
To receive – Ontvangen
Throughout – Door en door
Tonight - Vannacht
Through - Door
Him / his – Hem / zijn

I need to allow him to go with us.
Ik moet hem toestaan met ons mee te gaan.
He is a different man now.
Hij is nu een andere man.
I believe everything except for this
Ik geloof alles behalve dit
Come here quickly.
Kom vlug hier.
I can't recognize him.
Ik herken hem niet.
I need to put your cat to another chair
Ik moet je kat op een andere stoel leggen
I see the sun in the morning from the kitchen
Ik zie de zon in de ochtend vanuit de keuken
I go into the house from the front entrance and not through the yard.
Ik ga het huis binnen via de voordeur in plaats van de tuin.
I must go to sleep
Ik moet gaan slapen

To wish – Wensen
Bad - Slecht
To get – Krijgen
To forget – Vergeten
Everybody / Everyone - Iedereen
Although - Hoewel
To feel – Voelen
Great - Groot
Next - Volgende
To like – Leuk vinden
In front - Voor
Person - Persoon
Behind - Achter
Well - Goed
Restaurant - Restaurant
Bathroom - Toilet
Goodbye – Tot ziens

I don't want to wish anything bad
Ik wil je niet iets slechts wensen
I must forget everybody from my past.
Ik moet iedereen uit mijn verleden vergeten.
To feel well I must take vitamins
Om me goed te voelen, moet ik vitamines slikken.
I am close to the person behind you
Ik ben dichtbij de persoon achter jou
There is a great person in front of me
Er is een groot persoon voor mij
Goodbye my friend.
Vaarwel mijn vriend.
Which is the best restaurant in the area?
Wat is het beste restaurant in de buurt?
I can feel the heat.
Ik voel de warmte.
I need to repair a part of the cabinet in the bathroom.
Ik moet een deel van de badkamerkast repareren.
I want to buy car before the next year
Ik wil een auto voor het volgende jaar
I like the house, however it is very small
Ik wil dit huis leuk vinden, echter het is erg klein

To remove – Verwijderen
Please - Alsjeblieft
Beautiful - Mooi
To lift - Optillen
Include / Including - Inclusief
Belong – Behoren tot, horen
To hold – Houden
To check - Nakijken
Small - Klein
Real - Echt
Week - Week
Size – Maat, grootte
Even though - Hoewel
Doesn't - Niet
Price - Prijs

She wants to remove this door, please
Zij wil deze deur verwijderen, alsjeblieft
This doesn't belong here, I need to check again
Dit hoort hier niet, ik moet het opnieuw nakijken
This week the weather was very beautiful
Deze week was het weer erg mooi
Is that a real diamond?
Is dat een echte diamant?
We need to check the size of the house
We moeten de grootte van het huis nakijken
I want to lift this.
Ik wil dit optillen.
Can you please put the wood in the fire?
Kun je alsjeblieft het hout in het vuur gooien?
The sun is high in the sky.
De zon staat hoog aan de hemel.
Can you please hold my hand?
Kun je alsjeblieft mijn hand vasthouden?
I can pay this although the price is expensive
Ik kan dit betalen hoewel de prijs duur is
Including everything is this price correct?
Inclusief alles is deze prijs correct?

*In the sentence, "This week the weather was very beautiful" / *Deze week was het weer erg mooi*, "was"/*was* is the verb.

Building Bridges

In Building Bridges, we take six conjugated verbs that have been selected after studies I have conducted for several months in order to determine which verbs are most commonly conjugated, and which are then automatically followed by an infinitive verb. For example, once you know how to say, "I need," "I want," "I can," and "I like," you will be able to connect words and say almost anything you want more correctly and understandably. The following three pages contain these six conjugated verbs in first, second, third, fourth, and fifth person, as well as some sample sentences. Please master the entire program up until *here* prior to venturing onto this section.

I want – Ik wil
I need – Ik moet, Ik heb … nodig
I can – Ik kan
I like – Ik vind … leuk
I go – Ik ga
I have – Ik heb
I must – Ik moet

I want to go to my apartment
Ik wil naar mijn appartement gaan

I can go with you to the bus station
Ik kan met jou naar het busstation gaan

I need to walk outside the museum.
Ik moet buiten het museum lopen.

I like to eat oranges.
Ik eet graag sinaasappels.

I am going to teach a class
Ik ga een klas les geven

I have to speak to my teacher
Ik moet met mijn leraar spreken

Please master *every* single page up until here prior to attempting the following two pages!

You want / do you want?
Je wil / wil je?
He wants / does he want?
Hij wil / wil hij?
She wants / does she want?
Zij wil / wil zij?
We want / do we want?
We willen / willen we?
They want / do they want?
Zij willen / willen zij?
(Plural) You want / do you want?
Jullie willen / willen jullie?

You need / do you need?
Je hebt nodig / heb je nodig?
He needs / does he need?
Hij heeft nodig / heeft hij nodig?
She needs / does she need?
Zij heeft nodig / Heeft zij nodig?
We want / do we want?
We willen / willen we?
They need / do they need?
Zij hebben nodig / Hebben zij nodig?
(Plural) You need / do you need?
Jullie hebben nodig / hebben jullie nodig?

You can / can you?
Je kan / Kan je?
He can / can he?
Hij kan / kan hij?
She can / can she?
Zij kan / kan zij?
We can / can we?
We kunnen / kunnen we?
They can / can they?
Zij kunnen / kunnen zij?
(Plural) You can / can you?
Jullie kunnen / kunnen jullie?

You like / do you like?
Je vindt leuk / vind je leuk?
He likes / does he like?
Hij vindt leuk / vindt hij leuk?
She like / does she like?
Zij vindt leuk / vindt zij leuk?
We like / do we like?
We vinden leuk / vinden we leuk?
They like / do they like?
Zij vinden leuk / vinden zij leuk?
(Plural) You like / do you like?
Jullie vinden leuk / vinden jullie leuk?

You go / do you go?
Je gaat / ga je?
He goes / does he go?
Hij gaat / gaat hij?
She goes / does she go?
Zij gaat / gaat zij?
We go / do we go?
We gaan / gaan we?
They go / do they go?
Zij gaan / gaan zij?
(Plural) You go / do you go?
Jullie gaan / gaan jullie?

You have / do you have?
Je hebt / heb je?
He has / does he have?
Hij heeft / heeft hij?
She has / does she have?
Zij heeft / heeft zij?
We have / do we have?
We hebben / hebben we?
They have / do they have?
Zij hebben / hebben zij?
(Plural) You have / do you have?
Jullie hebben / hebben jullie?

Do you want to go?
Wil je gaan?

Does he want to fly?
Wil hij vliegen?

We want to swim
We willen zwemmen

Do they want to run?
Willen zij rennen?

Do you need to clean?
Moet je schoonmaken?
Moeten jullie schoonmaken?

She needs to sing a song
Zij moet een liedje zingen

We need to travel
We moeten reizen

You (plural) need to save your money.
Jullie moeten je geld sparen.

You (plural) need to see the film
Jullie moeten de film zien

Can you hear me?
Kan je me horen?

He can dance very well
Hij kan erg goed dansen

We can go out tonight
We kunnen vanavond uitgaan

The fireman can break the door during an emergency.
In een noodgeval kan de brandweerman de deur openbreken.

Do you like to eat here?
Vind je het leuk om hier te eten?

He likes to spend time here
Hij vindt het leuk om hier tijd door te brengen

We like to fix the house
We vinden het leuk om het huis te repareren

They like to cook
Zij vinden het leuk om te koken

You (plural) like to play soccer.
Jullie voetballen graag.

Do you go to the movies on weekends?
Ga je in het weekend naar de film?

He goes fishing
Hij gaat vissen

We are going to relax
Wij gaan uitrusten

They go out to eat at a restaurant every day.
Zij gaan dagelijks uit eten in een restaurant.

Do you have money?
Heb je geld?

She must look outside
Zij moet naar buiten kijken

We have to sign our names
We moeten onze namen tekenen

They have to send the letter
Zij moeten de brief sturen

You (plural) have to stand in line.
Jullie moeten in de rij aansluiten.

Days of the Week
Sunday - Zondag
Monday - Maandag
Tuesday - Dinsdag
Wednesday - Woensdag
Thursday - Donderdag
Friday - Vrijdag
Saturday - Zaterdag

Seasons
Spring – Lente, voorjaar / **Summer** - Zomer
Autumn - Herfst / **Winter** - Winter

Cardinal Directions
North Noord / **South** - Zuid
East - Oost / **West** – West

Colors
Black - Zwart
White - Wit
Gray - Grijs
Red - Rood
Blue - Blauw
Yellow - Geel
Green - Groen
Orange - Oranje
Purple - Paars
Brown - Bruin

Numbers
One - Één
Two - Twee
Three - Drie
Four - Vier
Five - Vijf
Six - Zes
Seven - Zeven
Eight - Acht
Nine - Negen
Ten – Tien

*"One" - *Één* - usually no accent on the capital, but when used in lower case, two accents: *één*.

Conversational Danish Quick and Easy
The Most Innovative Technique to Learn the Danish Language

YATIR NITZANY

The Danish Language

Danish, called *dansk*, is a North Germanic language spoken by around six million people, principally in Denmark and in the region of Southern Schleswig in northern Germany, where it has minority language status. It is also native to Greenland and the Faroe Islands.

Dialects include Bornholmian (Eastern Danish), South Jutlandic, and Insular Danish.

Danish uses the Dano-Norwegian alphabet and has a very large vowel inventory comprising twenty-seven phonemically distinctive vowels, and its patterns of stress and intonation are characterized by the distinctive phenomenon stød, a kind of laryngealization or creaky voice, which affects the utterance of a syllable by dividing it into two phases; a high first phase and drop in the second phase.

Danish is a descendant of Old Norse, which was the common language of the Germanic peoples who lived in Scandinavia during the Viking Era. A more recent classification based on mutual intelligibility separates modern spoken Danish, Norwegian, and Swedish as "mainland Scandinavian," while Icelandic and Faroese are classified as "insular Scandinavian."

Until the sixteenth century, Danish was a continuum of dialects with no standard variety or spelling conventions. A standard language was developed with the Protestant Reformation and the introduction of printing. It was based on the educated Copenhagen dialect and spread through use in the education system and administration. Following the loss of territory to Germany and Sweden, a nationalist movement adopted the language as a token of Danish identity. Today, traditional Danish dialects have all but disappeared, though regional variants of the standard language exist.

Reading and Pronunciation in Danish

Vowels (vokaler)

The Danish alphabet has nine vowels and each of these vowels can be either long, short, open or flat. Furthermore, Danish has three vowels that do not appear in the English alphabet Æ, Ø and Å. Below we will explain how each vowel can be pronounced

A (ah):

1. Der bor en **masse** mennesker (a lot of people are living there). Flat and short like the English 'flat'
2. Du skal ikke **mase** (Don't push). Flat and long like the English 'face'
3. Der står et **skab** (There is a closet). Very flat and long like the English 'make'
4. **Tak** for mad (Thank you for the food). Open and short like the English 'path'
5. Stræk dine **arme** (stretch your arms). Open and long like the English 'farmer'

E (eh):

1. Det er svært at stå på en **scene** (it is difficult to stand on a scene). Flat and long like the English '
2. Man kan bare **se** på (You can just look). Flat and short like the English 'dictionary'
3. Vi skal lige **tale** sammen (We have to talk). Short sound like the English 'open'
4. Han ligger i **sengen** (He is lying in bed). Long sound like the English 'men'

I (ee):

1. Hun er en god **kilde** (She is a good source). Flat and short like the English 'hill'
2. Følg den **sti** (follow that path). Flat and long like the English 'scream'
3. Det er et godt **minde** (it is a good memory). Open and short like the English 'link'

O (oh):

1. Det er et **foto** (It is a photo). Flat and short like the English 'botox'
2. Se min **kjole** (look at my dress). Flat and long like the English 'motor'

3. Bøgerne står på en **reol** (The books are on a bookshelf). Flat and very long like the English 'creole'
4. Jeg spiser ikke **ost** (I do not eat cheese). Short and pronounced like the English 'trophy'
5. Hun er ret **kort** (She is pretty short). Open and short like the English 'ball'

U (uh):

1. De er **fulde** af sjov (they are full of fun). Flat and short like the English 'bully'
2. De kiggede på **fuglene** (they were looking at the birds). Flat and long like the English 'moody'
3. Vi har nået **bunden** (We have reached bottom). Open and long like the English 'bungalow'

Y (eww):

1. Jeg **dysser** dem lidt ned (I'm calming them down a bit). Flat and short. No exact English equivalent.
2. Hun har ret **lys** hud (Her skin is pretty light). Flat and long like the English 'dew'
3. Han vil ikke **kysse** mig (He won't kiss me). Open and short. No exact English equivalent.
4. De **ryster** på hænderne (Their hands are shaking). Open and short pronounced like the English 'bird'

Æ (ai):

1. **Hælder** du lige op? (Will you please pour me a drink?). Pronounced like the English 'Let'
2. Jeg går i høje **hæle** (I'm wearing high heels). Pronounced like the English 'Make'
3. Vi **træffer** dem nok ikke (We will probably not meet them). Pronounced like the English 'arch'

Ø (oe):

1. Jeg vil gerne **købe** bilen (I want to buy the car). No exact English equivalent
2. Du må gerne **tørre** bordet (You can wipe the table). No exact English equivalent

Å (ou):

1. Jeg vil **låne** ham pengene (I want to lend him the money). Pronounced like the English 'mode'

2. Han har **dårlig ånde** (He has a bad breath). Pronounced like the English 'fault'

Diphthongs (diftonger)

In Danish, there are two main groups of diphthongs (when a vowel glide into another, e.g. like the English joy "joiee"). Can be spelled in many ways, but are all pronounced in the same way:

1. Diphthongs that ends in an i (ee)-sound
2. Diphthongs that ends in a u (oo)-sound

I (ee):

The **"AJ"-sound** (pronounced like the English I).

Der svømmer en **haj** (A shark is swimming there)

Jeg siger lige **hej** (I'm just going to say hello)

Han elsker **dig** (He loves you)

The **"ØJ"-sound** (pronounced like the English boy).

Han er **høj** (He is tall)

Jeg kan ikke lide **løg** (I do not like onions)

The **"AI"-sound** (pronounced like the English May)

Han er stadig **baby** (He is still a baby)

Du har fået **mail** (You've got mail)

I (ee):

The **"AV"-sound** (pronounced like the English now)

Vi sejler på det åbne **hav** (We are sailing at open sea)

Vi har en **aftale** (We have a deal)

The "IV"-sound (pronounced like the English eew)

Jeg har et godt **liv** (I have a good life)

The "OV"-sound (pronounced like the English or)

Han opfører sig som en **klovn** (He acts like a clown)

The "YV"-sound (pronounced like the English eew with rounded lips)

Vi mødes klokken **syv** (We will meet at seven)

The "ÆV"-sound (pronounced eoo)

Kaninen blev spist af en **ræv** (The rabbit was eaten by a fox)

The "ØV"-sound (like in the English though)

Hun havde fået nye **støvler** (She had gotten a new pair of boots)

Konsonanter (Consonants)
D (after a vowel) - Jeg sover på en **blød** pude (I sleep on a soft pillow). Like the English TH-sound.

DS - Det er min **hunds** halsbånd (The collar belongs to my dog). Silent.

G (between vowels)

Hun er en sød **pige** (She is a sweet girl). Often silent.

G (otherwise) - **Gulerødderne** er for **gamle** (The carrots are too old). Hard as in "get".

J - **Julen** bliver hvid i år (It is going to be a white Christmas this year). As the English Y.

K - **Køber** du lige aftensmad? (Will you please buy dinner?) Always a hard K as in the English "keep".

LD (final) - Jeg er **vild** med hende (I am crazy about her). Only pronounce the l-sound, as the d is silent.

ND (final) - Han er en god **mand** (He is a good man). Only pronounce the n-sound, as the d is silent.

R - Hun har **rød** kjole på (She is wearing a red dress). The Danish r-sound is pronounced from the throat.

RD (final) - Jeg bor på en stor **gård** (I live on a big farm). The d is silent here.

S - **Solen** skinner i dag (The sun is shining today). Always like the English sun or silent.

SJ - Det er **sjovt** at være i Tivoli (Going to Tivoli is fun). Like the English sh as in showbusiness.

ST,SP - **Står** du der og **spiller** smart? (Are you standing there acting tough?) Like in the English "standing" and "space".

V - **Vil** du med i biografen? (Would you like to go to the movies?). As in the English "wall".

Z - Der står en **zebra** i **zoo** (There is a zebra in the zoo). Like the English "sound".

I | I am - Jeg | Jeg er
With you – Med dig / (**Female/Flertal**) med jer
With him / with her – Med ham / med hende
With us – Med os
For you – For dig / (**Flertal**) for jer
Without him – Uden ham
Without them – Uden dem
Always - Altid
Was - Var
This - Den/det
Is - Er
Sometimes - Nogle gange
Today - I dag
Are you / you are – Er du / du er
Better - Bedre
You - Du/dig
You plural - I/jer
He / he is - Han/ han er
She / she is – Hun / hun er
From – Fra

Are you at the house?
Er du i huset?
I am always with her
Jeg er altid med hende
I am from the Denmark
Jeg kommer fra Danmark
Are you from Copenhagen?
Kommer du fra København?
I am with you
Jeg er med dig / (**Flertal**) jer
Are you alone today?
Er du alene i dag?
Sometimes I go without him.
Nogle gange går jeg uden ham.
This is for you
Det er for/til dig / (**Flertal**) jer

Flertal means "plural."

I was – Jeg var
To be - At være
The – Den / det
Same – Samme
Good – God/godt
Here - Her
It's / it is – Det er/den er
And - Og
Between - Mellem
Now - Nu
Later - Senere
After - Efter
If - Hvis
Yes - Ja
Then - Derefter/så
Very - Meget
Tomorrow - I morgen
Okay – OK/Okay
Also, too / as well - Også / såvel

I was home at 5pm
Jeg var hjemme ved 17-tiden

Between now and tomorrow.
Mellem nu og i morgen.

It's better to be home later.
Det er bedre at være hjemme senere.

If this is good, then I am happy.
Hvis dette er godt, så er jeg glad.

Yes, you are very good
Ja, du er meget god

I was here with them
Jeg var her med dem

The same day
Den samme dag

*In Danish "this" / "that" can either be *det* or *den*. *Det* relates to a situation in general, while *den* relates to a subject.

Maybe - Måske
Even if – Selvom
Afterwards – Bagefter / senere
Worse - Værre
Where - Hvor
Everything - Alting / alt
Somewhere - Et eller andet sted
What - Hvad
Almost - Næsten
There – Der / derhen

Even if I go now
Selvom jeg går nu

Where is everything?
Hvor er alt / alting?

Maybe somewhere
Måske et eller andet sted

What? I am almost there
Hvad? Jeg er næsten der

Where are you?
Hvor er du?

You and I
Du og jeg

Where is the airport?
Hvor er lufthavnen?

This is for us.
Dette er til os.

*In Danish, "everything" translates to either *alting* or *alt*.

*In the Danish language, *der* means "there," while *derhen* means "over there."

*This *isn't* a phrase book! The purpose of this book is *solely* to provide you with the tools to create *your own* sentences!

House / home - Et hus / hjem
In / at – I / på
Car - En bil
Already - Allerede
Good morning - God morgen
How are you? – Hvordan går det?
Where are you from? – Hvor kommer du fra?
Me – Mig (*Jeg* is a subject pronoun and *mig* is an object pronoun)
Hello - Hej
What is your name? – Hvad hedder du? / Hvad er dit navn?
How old are you? – Hvor gammel er du?
Son - En søn
Daughter - En datter
Your - Din / dit (both can be used interchangeably)
Hard - Hård / svært
Still – Stadig
But / however – Men / imidlertid
So *(as in then)* – Så

She is not in the car, so maybe she is still at the house?
Hun er ikke i bilen, så måske er hun stadig hjemme?
I am already in the car with your son and daughter
Jeg er allerede i bilen med din søn og datter
Good morning, how are you today?
God morgen, hvordan har du det i dag?
Hello, what is your name?
Hej, hvad hedder du? / Hej, hvad er dit navn?
How old are you?
Hvor gammel er du?
This is very hard, but it's not impossible
Det er meget svært, men ikke umuligt
Where are you from?
Hvor kommer du fra?

"He is" is *han er* / "she is" is / *hun er*, however, in questions, the verb and subject change position; "she is?"*er hun?* / "he is?" *er han?*
Ingen bil - "no car" / "without a car". *Bilen* - "the car." *En bil* - "a car."
*"Good morning" translates into *hvordan går det* or *hvordan har du det*. Both of which can be used interchangeably.
*In Danish *kommer* means "to come." "Are you from the Denmark?" can only be translated to *kommer du fra Danmark?*

Thank you – Tak/ tak skal du have
Thanks - Tak
For - For / til
A - En / et
This is – Det er / den er
Time - En tid
No / not - Nej / ikke
I am not – Jeg er ikke / det er jeg ikke
Away - Væk
That - Det / den / som
Similar - Lignede
Other/another – Anden/andet **(F)** andre; En anden / et andet
Side - Side
Until – Til / så længe / indtil
Yesterday - I går
Without us – Uden os
Since - Siden
Day - En dag
Before – Før
Late - Sent
Time / Times – Tid / tider
First – Første

Since the first time
Siden første gang
Thank you, Peter.
Tak, Peter.
It's almost time
Det er næsten tid
I am not here, I am far away
Jeg er her ikke, jeg er langt væk
That house is similar to ours.
Det hus ligner vores.
I am from the other side
Jeg er fra den anden side
But I was here until late yesterday
Men jeg var her indtil sent i går
Since the other day
Siden den anden dag

I say / I am saying - Jeg siger
I want – Jeg vil have (jeg vil gerne have)
Without you – Uden dig
Everywhere /wherever – Overalt / hvor som helst
I go / I am going – Jeg går
With - Med
My - Min / mit
Cousin - (**Male**) En fætter, (**Female**) en kusine
I need / I must – Jeg har brug for… / jeg må / jeg skal
Right now – Lige nu
Night - Aften/nat
To see - At se
Light - Et lys/lys
Outside - Udenfor
That is – Det/ den er
To be - At være
I see / I am seeing – Jeg ser

I am saying no / I say no
Jeg siger nej
I want to see this during the day
Jeg vil gerne se dette om dagen
I see this everywhere
Jeg ser det/den overalt
I am happy without any of my cousins here
Jeg er glad uden nogen af mine fætre her
I need to be there at night
Jeg skal være der om natten/aftenen
You need to be at home.
Du skal være hjemme.
I see the light outside
Jeg ser et lys udenfor

*_Gerne_ basically means "willingly" "with pleasure." "I want" _jeg vil_ however _jeg vil gerne_ sounds politer, however both phrases can be used.
*In Danish _skal_ means "must" "shall" while _er nødt til at_ means "need", _jeg vil_ means "I want" and _jeg vil gerne_ means "like". You will notice in the program these verbs will be used interchangeably.
*In Danish regarding the verb "need" _jeg har brug for_: "I need to"… (as in having a need for something) _jeg må_: "I may/must/have to" _jeg er nødt til_: "I need to" (it is necessary for me).

Place - En plads / et sted
Easy - Let / behagelig
To find – At finde
To look for / to search – At lede efter / at søge
Near / Close – Nær / tæt
Next to - Ved siden af
To wait – At vente
To sell – At sælge
To use – At bruge
To know – At vide
To decide – At afgøre / at beslutte
Between - Mellem
Two - To
To – Til / for / for at
That (conjunction) – At / fordi / for at

This place is easy to find
Dette sted er let at finde

I am saying to wait until tomorrow
Jeg siger, at du skal vente til i morgen

It's easy to sell this table
Det er let at sælge dette bord

I want to use this
Jeg vil gerne bruge det/den

Where is the book?
Hvor er bogen?

I need to look for you at the mall.
Jeg skal lede efter dig i indkøbscentret.

Is this place near?
Er dette sted i nærheden?

I need to know that everything is ok
Jeg er nødt til at vide, at alt er ok

*"Place" can mean both *en plads* or *et sted*. They are both interchangeable.

Because - Fordi
To buy – At købe
Both – Begge
Them / they / their - Dem / de / deres
Each - Hver
Every - Enhver
Book - En bog
Mine - Min / mine
To understand – At forstå
Problem / problems – Et problem / problemer
I do / I am doing – Jeg gør / jeg laver
Of – Af
To look – At kigge
Myself - Mig selv
Enough - Nok
Food – Mad
Water - Vand
Hotel - Et hotel

I like this hotel because it's near the beach
Jeg kan godt lide dette hotel, fordi det er tæt på stranden
I want to look at the view.
Jeg vil se på udsigten.
I want to buy a bottle of water
Jeg vil købe en flaske vand
Do it like this!
Gør det sådan her!
Both of them have enough food
De har begge nok mad
That book is mine.
Den bog er min.
I need to understand the problem
Jeg er nødt til at forstå problemet
I have a view of the city from the hotel
Jeg har et udsigt over byen fra hotellet
I do what I want.
Jeg gør hvad jeg vil.
I can work today
Jeg kan arbejde i dag

I like – Jeg kan godt lide...
There is / There are – Der er
Family – En familie
Parents – Forældre
Why - Hvorfor
To say – At sige
Something - Noget
To go – At gå
Ready - Klar
Soon – Snart
To work – At arbejde
Who? - Hvem?
Important – Vigtig
What time is it? – Hvad er klokken?

I like to be at home with my parents
Jeg kan godt lide at være hjemme med mine forældre

Why do I need to say something important?
Hvorfor skal jeg sige noget vigtigt?

I am there with him
Jeg er der med ham

I am busy, but I need to be ready soon
Jeg har travlt, men jeg skal være klar snart

I like to work
Jeg kan godt lide at arbejde

Who is there?
Hvem er der?

I want to know if they are here.
Jeg vil gerne vide, om de er her.

I can go outside.
Jeg kan gå udenfor.

There are seven dolls
Der er syv dukker

*With the knowledge you've gained so far, now try to create your own sentences!

How much - Hvor meget?
To take – At tage
With me – Med mig
Instead – I stedet for
Only - Kun
When - Hvornår
I can / can I? – Jeg kan / Må jeg?
Or - Eller
Were - Var
Without me – Uden mig
Fast - Hurtig
Slow - Langsom
Cold - Kold
Inside - Indenfor
To eat – At spise
Hot - Hed / varm
To Drive – At køre

How much money do I need to bring with me?
Hvor mange penge skal jeg have med?

I like bread instead of rice.
Jeg kan godt lide brød i stedet for ris.

Only when you can
Kun når du kan

Go there without me.
Gå derhen uden mig.

I need to drive the car very fast or very slowly
Jeg skal køre bilen meget hurtigt eller meget langsomt

It is cold in the library
Det er koldt på biblioteket

I like to eat a hot meal for my lunch.
Jeg kan godt lide at spise et varmt måltid til min frokost.

**Jeg kan lide* means "I like."

*The English word "when" translates into *hvornår* for asking a question. While *når* is used for the future or repeated situations.

To answer – At svare
To fly – At flyve
Today - I dag
To travel – At rejse
To learn – At lære
How - Hvordan
To swim – At svømme
To practice – At øve
To play – At spille
To leave – At forlade / *gå*
Many /much /a lot – Mange / meget / en masse
I go to – Jeg går til
To become - Bliver

I need to answer many questions
Jeg skal svare på mange spørgsmål
I want to fly today
Jeg vil flyve i dag
I need to learn to swim
Jeg skal lære at svømme
I want to learn how to play better tennis.
Jeg vil gerne lære at spille bedre tennis.
Everything is about the money.
Alt handler om pengene.
I want to leave my dog at home.
Jeg vil efterlade min hund derhjemme.
I want to travel the world.
Jeg vil rejse verden rundt.
The children are yours
Det er dine børn

*In Danish, you say "to **make** breakfast" and not "to prepare breakfast."

*På is a preposition (can be translated as: on, at, in, into, for), *svare på* – "answer to."

*Verden rundt translates to around the world. It can't be mirror translated.

*Both at *gå* and at *forlade* means "to leave" someone or something. *Forlade* is often used in cases where you want to emphasize that you are leaving for good or for a longer period of time.

Nobody / anyone - Ingen / nogen som helst
Against - Imod / mod
Us - Os
To visit – At besøge
Mom / Mother - En mor
To give – At give
Which – Hvilken / hvilket
To meet – At møde
Someone - Nogen
Just - Lige / netop/kun
To walk – At gå
Around - Rundt om
Towards - Hen imod
Than - End
Nothing – Ingenting

Something is better than nothing
Noget er bedre end ingenting
I am against him
Jeg er imod ham
We go each week to visit my family
Vi besøger min familie hver uge
I need to give you something
Jeg vil gerne give dig noget
Do you want to meet someone?
Vil du gerne møde nogen?
I am here also on Wednesdays
Jeg er her også om onsdagen
You do this everyday?
Gør du dette hver dag?
You need to walk around the school.
Du skal gå rundt på skolen.

*"Against" as in to (against the wall) is *imod* while "against" as in versus is *mod*.

*"Everything" is *alting*, "anything" is *noget*, "nothing" is *ingenting*.

Dig is the indirect object pronoun of the pronoun "you," the person who is actually affected by the action that is being carried out.

I have – Jeg har
Don't - Ikke
Friend - En ven
To borrow – At låne
To look like – At se ud som
To look like – At ligne
Grandfather – En bedstefar
To want – At ville have
To stay – At blive
To continue – At fortsætte
Way - En vej
Way - En retning
That's why - Derfor
To show – At vise
To prepare - At forberede
I am not going – Jeg tager ikke med

Do you want to look like Arnold?
Vil du ligne Arnold?

I want to borrow this book for my grandfather
Jeg vil låne denne bog til min bedstefar

I want to stay in Copenhagen because I have a friend there.
Jeg vil blive i København, fordi jeg har en ven der.

I don't want to see anyone here
Jeg vil ikke se nogen her

I need to show you how to prepare breakfast
Jeg skal vise dig, hvordan man laver morgenmad

Why don't you have the book?
Hvorfor har du ikke en bog?

That is incorrect, I don't need the car today
Det er forkert, jeg ikke har brug for bilen i dag

*This *isn't* a phrase book! The purpose of this book is *solely* to provide you with the tools to create *your own* sentences!

*"Correct" means *korrekt* while "incorrect" means *forkert*.

To remember – At huske
To sleep – At sove
Danish – Dansk
Number - Nummer
Hour - En time
Dark - Mørk
darkness – Et mørke
About – Om
Grandmother – En bedstemor
Five - Fem
Minute – Et minut
Minutes - Minutter
More - Mere
To think - At tænke
To do – At gøre
To come – At komme
To hear – At høre
Last – Sidste

Come here quickly.
Kom her hurtigt.

I need to remember your number
Jeg er nødt til at huske dit nummer

This is the last hour of darkness
Dette er den sidste time af mørket

I want to come with you.
Jeg vil gerne med dig.

I can hear my grandmother speaking Danish.
Jeg kan høre min bedstemor tale dansk.

I need to think about this more.
Jeg er nødt til at tænke mere over det her.

From here to there, it's only five minutes
Herfra og dertil tager det kun fem minutter

I must go to sleep
Jeg skal gå i seng

Again – Igen
Denmark - Danmark
To bring - At bringe
To try – At prøve
To rent – At leje
Without her – Uden hende
We are – Vi er
To turn off - At slukke
To ask – At spørge
To stop – At stoppe
Permission - Tilladelse

He must go and rent a house at the beach.
Han skal ud og leje et hus ved stranden.

We are here for a long time
Vi skal være her i lang tid

I need to turn off the lights early tonight
Jeg er nødt til at slukke lyset tidligt i aften

We want to stop here
Vi vil stoppe her

We are from Aarhus
Vi er fra Aarhus

Your doctor is in the same building.
Din læge er i samme bygning.

In order to leave you have to ask permission.
For at komme afsted skal du bede om tilladelse.

Our house is on the mountain.
Vores hus ligger på bjerget.

*In Danish *til*, *at*, *for at* means "to".

- *At bede om* / "to ask for"

- *En tilladelse til* **at** *forlade* / "a permission **to** leave"

*With the knowledge you've gained so far, now try to create your own sentences!

To open – At åbne
To buy – At købe
To pay – At betale
Last – Sidste
Without - Uden
Sister - En søster
To hope – At hoppe
To live – At leve / at bo
Nice to meet you – Rart at møde dig
Name - Et navn
Last name - Et efternavn
To return - At vende tilbage
Enough - Nok
Door - En dør

I need to open the door for my sister
Jeg er nødt til at åbne døren for min søster

I need to buy something
Jeg skal købe noget

I want to meet your brothers.
Jeg vil gerne møde dine brødre.

Nice to meet you, what is your name and your last name?
Rart at møde dig, hvad er dit navn og efternavn?

We can hope for a better future.
Vi kan håbe på en bedre fremtid.

It is impossible to live without problems.
Det er umuligt at leve uden problemer.

I want to return to the United States.
Jeg vil tilbage til USA.

Why are you sad right now?
Hvorfor er du ked af det nu?

*"To hope for" is different from "to hope". "To hope" is *at håbe*. "To hope for" is *at håbe på*.

To happen – At ske
To order – At bestille
To drink – At drikke
Excuse me – Undskyld mig
Child - Et barn
Woman - En kvinde
To begin / to start - At begynde / at starte
To finish – At færdiggøre
To help – At hjælpe
To smoke – At ryge
To love – At elske
To talk / to speak – At tale / at snakke

This needs to happen today
Det skal ske i dag
Excuse me, my child is here as well
Undskyld, mit barn er her også
I want to order a soup.
Jeg vil bestille en suppe.
We want to start the class soon.
Vi vil gerne starte klassen snart.
In order to finish at three o'clock this afternoon, I need to finish soon
For at blive færdig klokken tre i eftermiddag, skal jeg snart være færdig
I want to learn how to speak perfect Danish
Jeg vil gerne lære at tale perfekt dansk
I don't want to smoke again
Jeg vil ikke ryge igen
I love you
Jeg elsker dig
I see you
Jeg ser dig
I need you
Jeg har brug for dig
I want to help
Jeg vil gerne hjælpe

*"I don't want" is *jeg vil ikke*.
**Dig* is the direct object pronoun of the pronoun "you."

To read – At læse
To write – At skrive
To teach – At lære
To teach – At undervise
To close – At lukke
To turn on - At slukke
To prefer - At foretrække
To choose - At vælge
To put - At putte
To put - At sætte
To put - At lægge
Less - Mindre
Sun - En søn
Month - En måned
I talk – Jeg taler
Exact – Præcis

I need this book to learn how to read and write in Danish
Jeg har brug for denne bog for at lære at læse og skrive på dansk

I want to teach English in Denmark
Jeg vil gerne undervise i engelsk i Danmark

I want turn on the lights and close the door.
Jeg vil tænde lyset og lukke døren.

I want to pay less than you.
Jeg vil gerne betale mindre end dig.

I prefer to put this here.
Jeg foretrækker at sætte dette her.

I speak with the boy and the girl in German
Jeg taler med drengen og pigen på tysk

There is sun outside today.
Der er sol udenfor i dag.

Is it possible to know the exact date?
Er det muligt at kende den præcise dato?

*"Date" (time) is *dato*. However "to go on a date" is at *gå på en date*.

To exchange – At veksle / at udveksle / at bytte
To call – At ringe
Brother - En bror
Dad - En far
To sit – At sidde
Together - Sammen
To change – At forandre / at skifte
Of course – Naturligvis / selvfølgelig
Welcome - Velkommen
During - I løbet af / under
Years - Årene
Sky - En himmel
Up - Op
Down - Ned
Sorry - Undskyld / jeg er ked af det
To follow – At følge
Her – Hendes
Big - Stor
New - Ny
Never – Aldrig
His / hers – Hans / hendes

I am never able to exchange this money at the bank.
Jeg kan aldrig veksle disse penge i banken.
I want to call my brother and my dad today
Jeg vil ringe til min bror og min far i dag
Of course I can come to the theater, and I want to sit together with you and with your sister
Selvfølgelig kan jeg komme til teatret, og jeg vil sidde sammen med dig og med din søster
If you look under the table, you can see the new rug.
Kigger man under bordet, kan man se det nye tæppe.
I am sorry.
Det er jeg ked af.
The dog wants to follow me to the store.
Hunden vil følge mig til butikken.
I can see the sky from the window
Jeg kan se himlen fra vinduet
The dog wants to follow me to the store.
Hunden vil følge mig til butikken.

To allow - At give lov til
To believe – At tro
Morning - En morgen
Except - Undtagen
Except - Medmindre
To promise – At love
Good night - God nat
To recognize – At genkende
To recognize – At anerkende
People - Mennesker
To move – At flytte / at bevæge sig
Far - Langt / fjern
Different – Forskellig
Man - En mand
To enter – At gå ind
To receive – At få / at modtage
Throughout – Hele vejen igennem / helt igennem
Tonight - I aften / i nat
Through - Igennem
Him / his – Ham / hans

I need to allow him to go with us.
Jeg er nødt til at give ham lov til at tage med os.
He is a different man now.
Han er en anden mand nu.
I believe everything except for this
Jeg tror på alt undtagen det
I can't recognize him.
Jeg kan ikke genkende ham.
I need to put your cat to another chair
Jeg er nødt til at sætte din kat på en anden stol
I see the sun in the morning from the kitchen
Jeg ser solen om morgenen fra køkkenet
I want his car
Jeg vil have bil
I go into the house from the front entrance and not through the yard.
Jeg går ind i huset fra hovedindgangen og ikke gennem gården.

To wish – At ønske
Bad - Dårlig
To get – At få
To forget – At glemme
Everybody / Everyone - Enhver / alle / alle sammen
Although - Selvom
To feel – At føle
Great - Stor / dejlig
Next - Næste
To like – At kunne lide
In front - Foran
Person - En person
Behind - Bagefter
Behind - Bag
Well - Vel
Well - Godt
Restaurant - En restaurant
Bathroom - Et toilet
Goodbye – Farvel

I don't want to wish anything bad
Jeg vil ikke ønske noget dårligt
I must forget everybody from my past.
Jeg må glemme alle fra min fortid.
To feel well I must take vitamins
Jeg må tage vitaminer for at have det godt
There is a great person in front of me
Der er en dejlig person foran mig
Goodbye my friend.
Farvel min ven.
Which is the best restaurant in the area?
Hvilken er den bedste restaurant i området?
I can feel the heat.
Jeg kan mærke varmen.
I need to repair a part of the cabinet of the bathroom.
Jeg skal reparere en del af skabet på badeværelset.
I want a car before the next year
Jeg vil have en bil inden næste år
I like the house, but it is very small.
Jeg kan godt lide huset, men det er meget lille.

To remove – At fjerne
Please - Vær så venlig
Beautiful - Smuk
To lift - At løfte
Include / Including - At indeholde / inklusive
Belong – At tilhøre
To hold – At holde
To check - At tjekke
Small - Lille
Real - Ægte
Week - En uge
Size – En størrelse
Even though – Selvom
Doesn't - Ikke
So - Så
Price - En pris

She wants to remove this door, please
Hun vil fjerne denne dør, tak
This doesn't belong here, I need to check again
Dette tilhører ikke her, jeg er nødt til at tjekke igen
This week the weather was very beautiful
Denne uge var vejret meget smukt
Is that a real diamond?
Er det en rigtig diamant?
Kan du venligst holde min hånd?
We need to check the size of the house
Vi skal kontrollere husets størrelse
I want to lift this.
Jeg vil løfte dette.
The sun is high in the sky.
Solen står højt på himlen.
Can you please put the wood in the fire?
Kan du venligst lægge træet i ilden?
Can you please hold my hand?
Kan du venligst holde min hånd?
I can pay this although the price is expensive
Jeg kan betale for det, selvom prisen er dyr.

Building Bridges

In Building Bridges, we take six conjugated verbs that have been selected after studies I have conducted for several months in order to determine which verbs are most commonly conjugated, and which are then automatically followed by an infinitive verb. For example, once you know how to say, "I need," "I want," "I can," and "I like," you will be able to connect words and say almost anything you want more correctly and understandably. The following three pages contain these six conjugated verbs in first, second, third, fourth, and fifth person, as well as some sample sentences. Please master the entire program up until here prior to venturing onto this section.

I want – Jeg vil
I need – Jeg har brug for
I need – Jeg mangler
I need – Jeg er nødt til
I can – Jeg kan
I like – Jeg kan godt lide
I go – Jeg går
I have – Jeg har
I must – Jeg skal / jeg må

I want to go to my apartment
Jeg vil gerne hen til min lejlighed

I can go with you to the bus station
Jeg kan tage med dig til busstationen

I need to leave the museum.
Jeg skal forlade museet.

I like to eat oranges.
Jeg kan godt lide at spise appelsiner.

I am going to teach a class
Jeg skal undervise i en klasse

I have to speak to my teacher
Jeg skal snakke med min lærer

Please master *every* single page up until here prior to attempting the following pages!

You want / do you want?
Du vil / vil du?
He wants / does he want?
Han vil / vil han?
She wants / does she want?
Hun vil / vil hun?
We want / do we want?
Vi vil / vil vi?
They want / do they want?
De vil / vil de?
(Plural) You want/ do you want?
I vil / vil I?

You need / do you need?
Du har brug for… / har du brug for…?
He needs / does he need?
Han har brug for… / har han brug for…?
She needs / does she need?
Hun har brug for… / har hun brug for…?
We want / do we want?
Vi vil/ vil vi?
They need / do they need?
De har brug for… / har de brug for…?
(Plural) You need / do you need?
I har brug for… / har I brug for…?

You can / can you?
Du kan / Kan du?
He can / can he?
Han kan / kan han?
She can / can she?
Hun kan / kan hun?
We can / can we?
Vi kan/ kan vi?
They can / can they?
De kan/ kan de?
(Plural) You can / can you?
I kan / kan I?

You like / do you like?
Du kan godt lide / kan du godt lide?
He likes / does he like?
Han kan godt lide / kan han godt lide?
She like / does she like?
Hun kan godt lide / kan hun godt lide?
We like / do we like?
Vi kan godt lide/ kan vi godt lide?
They like / do they like?
De kan godt lide / kan de godt lide?
(Plural) You like / do you like?
I kan godt lide / kan I godt lide?

You go / do you go?
Du går / går du?
He goes / does he go?
Han går / går han?
She goes / does she go?
Hun går / går hun?
We go / do we go?
Vi går / går vi?
They go / do they go?
De går / går de?
(Plural) You go / do you go?
Du går / går du?

You have / do you have?
Du har / har du
He has / does he have?
Han har / har han?
She has / does she have?
Hun har / har hun?
We have / do we have?
Vi har/ har vi?
They have / do they have?
De har / har de?
(Plural) You have / do you have?
I har / har I?

Do you want to go?
Vil du gerne gå?

Does he want to fly?
Vil han gerne flyve?

We want to swim
Vi vil gerne svømme

Do they want to run?
Vil de gerne løbe?

Do you need to clean?
Er du nødt til at gøre rent?

She needs to sing a song
Hun har brug for at synge en sang

We need to travel
Vi er nødt til at rejse

They don't need to fight
De behøver ikke at kæmpe

You (plural) need to save your money.
I skal spare på jeres penge.

Can you hear me?
Kan du høre mig?

He can dance very well
Han kan danse meget godt

The fireman can break the door during an emergency.
Brandmanden kan bryde døren op under en nødsituation.

They can break the wood
De kan knække træet

Do you like to eat here?
Kan du lide at spise her?

He likes to spend time here
Han kan lide at bruge tid her

We like to fix the house
Vi kan godt lide at reparere huset

They like to cook
De elsker at lave mad

You (plural) like to play soccer.
I kan lide at spille fodbold.

Do you go to the movies on weekends?
Går du i biografen i weekenden?

He goes fishing
Han tager på fisketur

We are going to relax
Vi skal slappe af

They go out to eat at a restaurant every day.
De går ud og spiser på en restaurant hver dag.

Do you have money?
Har du penge?

She must look outside
Hun er nødt til at kigge udenfor

We have to sign our names
Vi skal underskrive vores navne

They have to send the letter
De skal sende brevet

You (plural) have to stand in line.
I skal stå i kø.

Other Useful Tools in the Danish Language

Days of the Week

Sunday - Søndag
Monday - Mandag
Tuesday - Tirsdag
Wednesday - Onsdag
Thursday - Torsdag
Friday - Fredag
Saturday - Lørdag

Seasons

Spring – Forår
Summer - Sommer
Autumn - Efterår
Winter - Vinter

Colors

Black - Sort
White - Hvid
Gray - Grå
Red - Rød
Blue - Blå
Yellow - Gul
Green - Grøn
Orange - Orange
Purple - Lilla
Brown - Brun

Cardinal Directions

North - Nord
South - Syd
East - Øst
West –Vest

Numbers

One – En
Two – To
Three – Tre
Four – Fire
Five – Fem
Six – Seks
Seven – Syv
Eight – Otte
Nine – Ni
Ten – Ti
Eleven – Elleve
Twelve – Tolv
Thirteen – Tretten
Fourteen – Fjorten
Fifteen – Femten
Sixteen – Seksten
Seventeen – Sytten
Eighteen – Atten
Nineteen – Nitten
Twenty – Tyve
Thirty – Tredive
Forty – Fyrre
Fifty – Halvtreds
Sixty – Tres
Seventy – Halvfjerds
Eighty – Firs
Ninety – Halvfems
Hundred – Hundred
Thousand – Tusind
Million – Million
Billion – Milliard

Conversational Norwegian Quick and Easy
The Most Innovative Technique to Learn the Norwegian Language

YATIR NITZANY

The Norwegian Language

Norwegian (*Norsk*) is the official language of Norway and is a North Germanic language (along with Faroese, Icelandic, Swedish, and Danish) that is mainly only spoken there. The languages of Norway, Sweden, and Denmark are similar and in most cases you can speak Norwegian to Danes and Swedes, and also read text written in Swedish and Danish.

The two official forms of written Norwegian are *Bokmål* (literally "book tongue," the form used in this book) and *Nynorsk* (literally "new Norwegian"). Nynorsk and Bokmål provide standards for how to write Norwegian, but not for how to speak the language. No standard of spoken Norwegian is officially sanctioned, and most Norwegians speak their own dialects in all circumstances.

There are two other written forms of Norwegian, *Riksmål* ("state language") and *Høgnorsk* ("High Norwegian"). These are without official status. Riksmål, is today to a large extent the same language as Bokmål though somewhat closer to the Danish language. The other is a more purist form of Nynorsk, which in an effort to maintain the language in an original form rejects most of the reforms from the twentieth century; this form has limited use.

From the sixteenth to the nineteenth centuries, Danish was the standard written language of Norway. Historically, Bokmål is a Norwegianised variety of Danish, while Nynorsk is a language form based on Norwegian dialects and purist opposition to Danish.

Norwegians are educated in both Bokmål and Nynorsk. The majority use primarily Bokmål as their daily written language, while a small percentage use both Bokmål and Nynorsk, and others use primarily Nynorsk.

Reading and Pronunciation in Norwegian

a – "ah" as in father

e – "eh" as in men

i – "ee" as in see

o – "ooh" as in pool

u – no real equivalent in English, but a bit like the "e" in new

y – no equivalent in English, something in between "I" and "u"

æ – as the "a" in bad

ø – no equivalent in English, but is pronounced as 'eux' in the French word 'deux'

å – "awe" as in saw

j – like the "y" in you

kj – no equivalent in English, but like the 'x' in Mexico (in Spanish)

sj/skj – "sh" as in she

ei/eg (end of words) – as the "igh" in light and high

ig (end of words) – as the "y" in nicely

The *t* and *d* are not pronounced if they are the last letters of the word.

The Program

I / I am - Jeg | Jeg er
With you – Med deg / (**Plural**) med dere
With him – Med han
With her – Med henne
With us – Med oss
For you – Til deg / (**Plural**) til dere
Without him – Uten han
Without them – Uten henne
Always - Alltid
Was - Var
This - Dette
Is - Er
Sometimes – Noen ganger
Today – I dag
Are you / you are – Er du, Er dere
Better - Bedre
You - Du, deg / **You (plural)** - Dere
He – Han
She – Hun
From - Fra

Are you at the house?
Er du ved huset?
I am always with her
Jeg er alltid med henne
I am from Norway
Jeg er fra Norge
Are you from Oslo?
Er du fra Oslo?
I am with you
Jeg er med deg, (pl.) dere
Are you alone today?
Er du alene i dag?
This is for you
Dette er til deg (Pl.) dere
Sometimes I go without him.
Noen ganger går jeg uten ham.

I was – Jeg var
To be – Å være
The – En/ei/et
Good – God, bra
Here - Her
It's / it is – Det er
And - Og
Between - Mellom
Now - Nå
Later / After – Senere, etter
If - Hvis
Yes - Ja
Then - Da
Tomorrow – I morgen
Okay - OK
Also / too / as well - Også

I was home at 5pm
Jeg var hjemme klokken 17
Between now and tomorrow.
Mellom nå og i morgen.
It's better to be home later.
Det er bedre å være hjemme senere.
If this is good, then I am happy.
Hvis dette er bra, så er jeg fornøyd.
Yes, you are very good
Ja, du er veldig bra
I was here with them
Jeg var her med dem

*In the Norwegian language the masculine form of the article "the" is *en*, the feminine form is *ei*, and the neuter form is *et*. These forms become suffixes to the noun. It's sometimes hard to decipher whether a noun is masculine or feminine in the Norwegian language, so most people who study this language memorize the article as they go along.

*To make an article definite in Norwegian, you add it a suffix to the noun. For example: "A day" *en dag* /"The day" *dagen*. Feminine words can be treated in two ways; either by adding *–en* or *–a* after the word. For example: "A daughter" *ei datter* / "The daughter" *datteren* or *dattera*. To make plural noun definite, add *–ene* behind the word. For example: "A house" *et hus* / "The houses" *husene* / "A day" *en dag* / "The days" *dagene*.

Maybe - Kanskje
You – Du, deg
Even if – Selv om
Afterwards - Etterpå
Worse - Verre
Where - Hvor
Everything - Alt
Somewhere – Noen plass, et sted
What - Hva
Almost - Nesten
There - Der

Even if I go now
Selv om jeg går nå
Where is everything?
Hvor er alt?
Maybe somewhere
Kanskje et sted
What? I am almost there
Hva? Jeg er nesten der
Where are you?
Hvor er du?
You and I
Du og jeg
Where is the airport?
Hvor er flyplassen?
This is for us.
Dette er for oss.

*In Norwegian, "you" could either translate *du, deg, de* or *dem*
Du is the nominative informal "you" (*de* is the formal), *deg* is the accusative "you" (formal: *dem*), and *deg* is the dative "you" (formal: *dem*).
Nominative simply means "you." "You are Norwegian?" / *du er norsk?*
Accusative is the direct object:
"I see you" / *jeg ser deg* or "I love you" / *jeg elsker deg*
Dative is the indirect object in the sentence (from someone / to someone / for someone):
"I must give you" / *jeg må gi deg* / "I want to show you" / *jeg vil vise deg*
Plural "you":
Nominative informal: *dere* / Accusative informal: *dere* / Dative is *dere*

House - Hus
Home - Hjemme
In / at – I / på
Car - Bil
Already - Allerede
Good morning – God morgen
How are you? – Hvordan går det?
Where are you from? – Hvor er du fra?
Me - Meg
Hello - Hei
What is your name? – Hva er ditt navn?
How old are you? – Hvor gammel er du?
Son - Sønn
Daughter - Datter
Your – Din / ditt / dine
Very - Veldig
Hard - Vanskelig
Still - Fortsatt
For – Til, for

She is not in the car, so maybe she is still at the house?
Hun er ikke i bilen, så kanskje hun fortsatt er i huset?
I am already in the car with your son and daughter
Jeg er allerede i bilen med din sønn og datter
Good morning, how are you today?
God morgen, hvordan går det i dag?
Hello, what is your name?
Hei, hva er ditt navn?
How old are you?
Hvor gammel er du?
This is very hard, but it's not impossible
Dette er veldig vanskelig, men det er ikke umulig
Where are you from?
Hvor er du fra?

*In Norwegian, "for" is usually translated as *til*, and sometimes as *for* or *om*. There are also other options depending on the sentence.

*In Norwegian, in the event that a sentence begins with an adverb, the subject and verb change positions in the sentence.

A (article) – En, ei, et
This is – Dette er
Time - Tid
But / however – Men / derimot
No / not – Nei / ikke
I am not – Jeg er ikke
Away - Borte
That - Det
Similar - Lignende
Other / Another - Annen
Side - Side
Until - Inntil
Yesterday – I går
Without us – Uten oss
Since - Siden
Day - Dag
Before - Før
Almost – Nesten

It's almost time
Det er nesten tid

I am not here, I am far away
Jeg er ikke her, jeg er langt unna

That house is similar to ours.
Det huset ligner på vårt.

I am from the other side
Jeg er fra den andre siden

But I was here until late yesterday
Men jeg var het til sent i går

Since the other day
Siden den andre dagen

*This *isn't* a phrase book! The purpose of this book is *solely* to provide you with the tools to create *your own* sentences!

*Prepositions in Norwegian are extremely difficult. "For" will most of the time be translated as *til*, but in combination with "thanks"/*takk* it is always translated as "for."

I say / I am saying – Jeg sier
What time is it? – Hva er klokka?
I want – Jeg vil
Without you – Uten deg
Everywhere /wherever – Overalt
I go / I am going – Jeg går
With - Med
My – Min, mitt, mine
Cousin – Kusine, (**Male**) Nevø, (**Female**) Niese
I need / I must – Jeg trenger / Jeg må
Right now – Akkurat nå
Night - Natt
To see – Å se
Light - Lys
Outside - Ute
That is – Det er
To be – Å være
I see / I am seeing – Jeg ser

I am saying no / I say no
Jeg sier nei
I want to see this during the day
Jeg vil se dette i løpet av dagen
I see this everywhere
Jeg ser dette overalt
I am happy without any of my cousins here
Jeg er lykkelig uten noen av søskenbarna mine her
I need to be there at night
Jeg trenger å være det om natten
You need to be at home.
Du må være hjemme.
I see light outside
Jeg ser lys ute
What time is it right now?
Hva er klokka akkurat nå?

*Concerning the sentence "I want to see this during the day"/ *Jeg vil se dette i løpet av dagen*. If you want to say that you want to see it during the upcoming day, it is translated as *i løpet av*. If you mean you want to see it during the day and not in the evening or night, it is translated as *Jeg vil se dette om dagen*.

Easy - Lett
To find – Å finne
To look for / to search – Å lete etter / Å søke
To wait – Å vente
To sell – Å selge
To use – Å bruke
To know – Å vite
To decide – Å bestemme
Between - Mellom
Two - To
To – Til
Myself – Meg
That *(conjunction)* - At

This place is easy to find
Denne plassen er lett å finne
I am saying to wait until tomorrow
Jeg sier å vente til i morgen
It's easy to sell this table
Det er lett å selge dette bordet
I want to use this
Jeg vil bruke dette
Where is the book?
Hvor er boken?
I need to look for you at the mall.
Jeg må se etter deg på kjøpesenteret.
I need to know that everything is ok
Jeg trenger å vite at alt er ok

*In Norwegian prepositions are extremely difficult as most of them have no logical explanation and are just part of an expression. For example, when talking about where someone is from, you would say in Norwegian "I live in Oslo" / *Jeg bor i Oslo* because it is a big city, but when you are from a small town, you say "I live on Hjelset" / *Jeg bor på Hjelset*. Don't stress about the prepositions, many Norwegians don't know which one is correct in every case either.

**Ved siden av* is a fixed expression that means "next to." If you use *nær*, it means "close to" and if you use *ved* it also means "close to" or "around."

Because - Fordi
To buy – Å kjøpe
Both - Begge
Them / they / their – Dem / de / deres
Each / Every – Hver, hvert / alle
Book - Bok
Mine – Min, mitt
To understand – Å forstå
Problem / Problems – Problem / Problemer
Of - Av
To look – Å se
Enough - Nok
Food - Mat
Water - Vann
Hotel - Hotell

I like this hotel because it's near the beach
Jeg liker dette hotellet fordi det er nær stranden
I want to look at the view.
Jeg vil se på utsikten.
I want to buy a bottle of water
Jeg vil kjøpe en flaske vann
Do it like this!
Gjør det slik!
Both of them have enough food
Begge av de har nok mat
That book is mine.
Den boka er min.
I need to understand the problem
Jeg trenger å forstå problemet
I can work today
Jeg kan jobbe i dag

*In Norwegian *over* is a preposition that cannot really be explained.

*If you notice in the sentence "I want to buy a bottle of water" / *Jeg vil kjøpe en flaske vann*, "of"/*av*, isn't used. The use of "of" is usually not translated (same as in Dutch and German).

I like – Jeg liker
There is – Der er
There are – Der er
Family - Familie,
Parents - Foreldre
Why - Hvorfor
To say – Å si
Something - Noe
To go – Å gå
Ready - Ferdig
Soon - Snart
To work – Å jobbe
Who - Hvem
Important - Viktig
Same – Samme, lik

I like to be at home with my parents
Jeg liker å være hjemme med mine foreldre

Why do I need to say something important?
Hvorfor trenger jeg å si noe viktig?

I am there with him
Jeg er der med han

I am busy, but I need to be ready soon
Jeg er opptatt, men jeg trenger å være ferdig snart

I like to work
Jeg liker å jobbe

I want to know if they are here.
Jeg vil vite om de er her.

I can go outside.
Jeg kan gå ut.

The same day
Den samme dagen

There are seven dolls
Der er sju/syv dukker

How much – Hvor mye
To take – Å ta
With me – Med meg
Instead – I stedet for, istedenfor
Only – Kun, bare
When - Når
I can / Can I? – Jeg kann
I can / Can I? – Kann jeg?
Or - Eller
Were - Var
Without me – Uten meg
Fast – Fort, rask
Slow - Sakte
Cold - Kalt
Inside - Inne
To eat – Å spise
Hot - Varm
To Drive – Å kjøre

How much money do I need to bring with me?
Hvor mye penger må jeg ha med meg?
I like bread instead of rice.
Jeg liker brød i stedet for ris.
Only when you can
Bare hvis du kann
Go there without me.
Gå dit uten meg.
I need to drive the car very fast or very slowly
Jeg trenger å kjøre bilen veldig fort eller veldig sakte
It is cold in the library
Det er kaldt på biblioteket
I like to eat a hot meal for my lunch.
Jeg liker å spise et varmt måltid til lunsj.

*In Norwegian, whenever asking a question, the pronoun follows the conjugated verb. As you can see in the first sentence: "how much money do I need to take?" / *Hvor mye penger trenger jeg å ta?* The pronoun *jeg* / "I" follows the conjugated verb *trenger* / "I need."

To answer – Å svare, å besvare
To fly – Å fly
Today – I dag
To travel – Å reise
To learn – Å lære
How - Hvordan
To swim – Å svømme
To practice – Å øve
To play – Å leke, å spille
To leave – Å la, å forlate
Many /much /a lot – Mange / mye / mange
I go to – Jeg går til, jeg skal
First - Først
Time / Times – Tid / tider

I need to answer many questions
Jeg trenger å besvare mange spørsmål

I want to fly today
Jeg vil fly i dag

I need to learn to swim
Jeg trenger å lære å svømme

I want to learn how to play better tennis.
Jeg vil lære å spille bedre tennis.

Everything is about the money.
Alt handler om pengene.

I want to leave my dog at home.
Jeg vil la hunden min være hjemme.

I want to travel the world.
Jeg vil reise rundt i verden.

Since the first time
Siden den første tiden

The children are yours
Barna er dine

*With the knowledge you've gained so far, now try to create your own sentences!

Thank you – Takk / Tusen takk
Nobody – Ingen
Anyone - hvem som helst
Against – Imot
Us - Oss
To visit – Å besøke
Mom / Mother – Mama, mor
To give – Å gi
Which - Hvilke
To meet – Å møte
Someone - Noen
Just - Akkurat
To walk – Å gå
Around - Rundt
Towards - Mot
Than - Enn
Nothing – Ingenting

Thank you, Peter.
Takk, Peter.

Something is better than nothing
Noe er bedre enn ingenting

I am against him
Jeg er imot han

We go each week to visit my family
Vi besøker min familie hver uke

I need to give you something
Jeg trenger å gi deg noe

Do you want to meet someone?
Vil du møte noen?

I am here also on Wednesdays
Jeg er her også på onsdager

You do this every day?
Du gjør dette hver dag?

You need to walk around the school.
Du må gå rundt skolen.

I have – Jeg har
Don't - Ikke
Friend - Venn
To borrow – Å låne
To look like – Å se ut som
Grandfather - Bestefar
To want – Å ville
To stay – Å bli
To continue – Å fortsette
Way - Vei
That's why - Derfor
To show – Å vise
To prepare – Å forberede, å lage
I am not going – Jeg skal ikke

Do you want to look like Arnold?
Vil du se ut som Arnold?

I want to borrow this book for my grandfather
Jeg vil låne denne boken for min bestefar

I want to stay in Oslo because I have a friend there.
Jeg vil bo i Trondheim fordi jeg har en venn der.

I don't want to see anyone here
Jeg vil ikke se noen her

I need to show you how to prepare breakfast
Jeg trenger å vise deg hvordan å lage frokost

Why don't you have the book?
Hvorfor har du ikke boken?

That is incorrect, I don't need the car today
Det er ikke korrekt, jeg trenger ikke bilen i dag

*In Norwegian, "don't" comes after the verb: "I don't need" / *jeg trenger ikke.*

*In Norwegian, you would say "to **make** breakfast" and not "to prepare breakfast."

*This *isn't* a phrase book! The purpose of this book is *solely* to provide you with the tools to create *your own* sentences!

To remember – Å huske
Norwegian - Norsk
Number - Nummer
Hour - Time
Dark – Mørk
Dark – Mørke
About – Om, på
Grandmother - Bestemor
Place - Plass
Near / Close - Nær
Five - Fem
Minute – Minutt
Minutes – Minutter
More - Mer
To think – Å tenke
To do – Å gjøre
To come – Å komme
To hear – Å høre
Last - Sist

I need to remember your number
Jeg trenger å huske ditt nummer

This is the last hour of darkness
Dette er den siste timen mørke

I want to come with you.
Jeg vil bli med deg.

I can hear my grandmother speaking Norwegian.
Jeg kan høre bestemoren min snakke norsk.

I need to think about this more.
Jeg må tenke mer på dette.

We are from Norway.
Vi er fra Norge.

From here to there, it's only five minutes
Fra her til der, er det bare fem minutter

Is this place near?
Er dette stedet i nærheten?

To leave – Å dra
Again - Igjen
Norway - Norge
To bring – Å levere, å ta med
To try – Å prøve
To rent – Å leie
Without her – Uten henne
We are – Vi er
To turn off – Å slå av
To ask – Å spørre
To stop – Å stoppe
I do / I am doing – Jeg gjør
Permission - Tillatelse
Goodbye – Ha det bra
Goodbye – Farvel

He must go and rent a house at the beach.
Han må gå og leie et hus på stranden.

We are here for a long time
Vi er her i lang tid

I need to turn off the lights early tonight
Jeg trenger å slå av lyset tidlig i kveld

We want to stop here
Vi vil stoppe her

We are from Bergen
Vi er fra Bergen

Your doctor is in the same building.
Legen din er i samme bygning.

In order to leave you have to ask permission.
For å dra må du spørre om tillatelse.

I do what I want.
Jeg gjør som jeg vil.

Goodbye my friend.
Ha det bra min venn.

To open – Å åpne
To buy – Å kjøpe
To pay – Å betale
Last - Sist
Without - Uten
Sister - Søster
To hope – Å håpe
To live – Å bo, å leve
Nice to meet you – Hyggelig å møte deg
Name - Navn
Last name - Etternavn
To return – Å retunere
Enough - Nok
Door - Dør

I need to open the door for my sister
Jeg trenger å åpne døren for min søster

I need to buy something
Jeg trenger å kjøpe noe

I want to meet your brothers.
Jeg vil møte brødrene dine.

Nice to meet you, what is your name and your last name?
Hyggelig å møte deg, hva er ditt navn og ditt etternavn?

To hope for the better in the future
Jeg håper på det beste i framtiden

We can hope for a better future.
Vi kan håpe på en bedre fremtid.

It is impossible to live without problems.
Det er umulig å leve uten problemer.

I want to return to the United States.
Jeg vil tilbake til USA.
Jeg vil returnere fra USA

Why are you sad right now?
Hvorfor er du trist akkurat nå

To happen – Å skje
To order – Å bestille
To drink – Å drikke
Excuse me - Unnskyld
Child - Barn
Woman - Kvinne
To begin / to start – Å starte
To finish – Å bli ferdig
To help – Å hjelpe
To smoke – Å røyke
To love – Å elske
To talk / to speak – Å snakke

This must happen today
Dette må skje i dag
Excuse me, my child is here as well
Unnskyld, mitt barn er her også
I want to order a soup.
Jeg vil bestille en suppe.
We want to start the class soon.
Vi ønsker å starte timen snart.
In order to finish at three o'clock this afternoon, I need to finish soon.
For å komme i mål til klokken tre i ettermiddag, må jeg bli ferdig snart.
I want to learn how to speak perfect Norwegian.
Jeg vil lære å snakke perfekt norsk.
I don't want to smoke again.
Jeg vil ikke røyke igjen.
I love you.
Jeg elsker deg.
I see you.
Jeg ser deg.
I need you
Jeg trenger deg
I want to help
Jeg vil hjelpe

*I don't want" is *jeg vil ikke*

To read – Å lese
To write – Å skrive
To teach – Å lære, å undervise
To close – Å lukke
To turn on – Å slå på
To prefer / to choose – Å foretrekke
To put – Å legge
Less – Mindre, færre
Sun - Sol
Month - Måned
I talk – Jeg snakker
Exact – Akkurat, eksakt
Our - Vårt
On - På

I need this book to learn how to read and write in Norwegian.
Jeg trenger denne boken for å lære å lese og skrive på norsk.

I want to teach English in Norway.
Jeg ønsker å undervise i engelsk i Norge.

I want turn on the lights and close the door.
Jeg vil slå på lyset og lukke døren.

I want to pay less than you.
Jeg vil betale mindre enn deg.

I prefer to put this here.
Jeg foretrekker å legge dette her.

I speak with the boy and the girl in German
Jeg snakker med gutten of jenta på tysk

There is sun outside today.
Det er sol ute i dag.

Is it possible to know the exact date?
Er det mulig å vite den eksakte datoen?

Our house is on the mountain
Vårt hus er på bakken

I must go to sleep
Jeg må legge meg

To exchange – Å bytte, å veksle
To call – Å ringe
Brother - Bror
Dad - Far
To sit – Å sitte
Together - Sammen
To change – Å endre
Of course - Selvfølgelig
Welcome - Velkommen
During - Mens
Years - År
Sky - Himmel
Up - Opp
Down - Ned
Sorry - Beklager
To follow – Å følge
Her – Henne, hennes
Big - Stor
New - Ny
Never – Aldri
His – Hans
Hers – Hennes

I am never able to exchange this money at the bank.
Jeg kan aldri veksle disse pengene i banken.
I want to call my brother and my dad today
Jeg vil ringe min bror og min far i dag
Of course I can come to the theater, and I want to sit together with you and with your sister
Selvfølgelig kan jeg komme til teateret, og jeg vil sitte sammen med deg og med din søster
If you look under the table, you can see the new rug.
Ser du under bordet kan du se det nye teppet.
I am sorry.
Jeg beklager.
I can see the sky from the window
Jeg kan se himmelen fra vinduet
The dog wants to follow me to the store.
Hunden vil følge meg til butikken.

To allow – Å tillate
To believe – Å tro
Morning - Morgen
Except – Bortsett fra
To promise – Å love
Good night – God natt
To recognize – Å gjenkjenne
People - Mennesker
To move – Å bevege
Far - Langt
Different – Forskjellig, annen
Man - Mann
To enter – Å gå inn
To receive – Å motta
Throughout - Gjennom
Tonight – I kveld
Through - Gjennom
Him – Han
His – Hans

I need to allow him to go with us.
Jeg må la ham å bli med oss.
He is a different man now.
Han er en annen mann nå.
I believe everything except for this
Jeg tror alt bortsett fra dette
Come here quickly.
Kom hit raskt.
I can't recognize him.
Jeg kan ikke kjenne ham igjen.
I need to put your cat to another chair.
Jeg trenger å legge din katt på en annen stol.
I see the sun in the morning from the kitchen.
Jeg ser solen om morgenen fra kjøkkenet.
I go into the house from the front entrance and not through the yard.
Jeg går inn i huset fra inngangen foran og ikke gjennom hagen.

*With the knowledge you've gained so far, now try to create your own sentences!

To wish – Å ønske
Bad - Dårlig
To get – Å få
To forget – Å glemme
Everybody – Alle
Everyone – Alle
Although – Selv om
To feel – Å føle
Great - Stor
Next - Neste
To like – Å like
In front - Foran
Person - Person
Behind - Bak
Well - Bra
Restaurant - Restaurant
Bathroom - Toalett

I don't want to wish anything bad
Jeg vil ikke ønske noe dårlig
I must forget everybody from my past.
Jeg må glemme alle fra fortiden min.
To feel well I must take vitamins
For å føle meg bra må jeg ta vitaminer
I am next to the person behind you
Jeg er nær personen bak deg
There is a great person in front of me
Det er en stor person foran meg
Which is the best restaurant in the area?
Hvilken er den beste restauranten i området?
I can feel the heat.
Jeg kan føle varmen.
I need to repair a part of the cabinet of the bathroom.
Jeg må reparere en del av skapet på badet.
I want a car before the next year
Jeg vil ha en bil før neste år
I like the house, but it is very small.
Jeg liker huset, men det er veldig lite.

To remove – Å fjerne
Please – Vær så snill
Beautiful - Pen
To lift – Å løfte
Include / Including - Inkludert
Belong – Høre til
To hold – Å holde
To check – Å sjekke
To sleep – Å sove
Small - Lite
Real - Ekte
Week - Uke
Size - Størrelse
Even though – Selv om
Doesn't - Ikke
So - Så
Price - Pris

She wants to remove this door, please
Hun vil fjerne denne døren, vær så snill
This doesn't belong here, I need to check again
Dette hører ikke til her, jeg må sjekke igjen
This week the weather was very beautiful
Denne uken var været veldig pent
Is that a real diamond?
Er det en ekte diamant?
We need to check the size of the house
Vi trenger å sjekke størrelsen på huset
I want to lift this.
Jeg vil løfte dette.
The sun is high in the sky.
Solen står høyt på himmelen.
Can you please put the wood in the fire?
Kan du være så snill å legge veden på bålet?
Can you please hold my hand?
Kan du være så snill å holde hånden min?
I can pay this although the price is expensive
Jeg kan betale dette selv om prisen er dyr

Building Bridges

In Building Bridges, we take six conjugated verbs that have been selected after studies I have conducted for several months in order to determine which verbs are most commonly conjugated, and which are then automatically followed by an infinitive verb. For example, once you know how to say, "I need," "I want," "I can," and "I like," you will be able to connect words and say almost anything you want more correctly and understandably. The following three pages contain these six conjugated verbs in first, second, third, fourth, and fifth person, as well as some sample sentences. Please master the entire program up until *here* prior to venturing onto this section.

I want – Jeg vil
I need – Jeg trenger
I can – Jeg kan
I like – Jeg liker
I go – Jeg går, jeg skal
I have - Jeg har
I must – Jeg må

I want to go to my apartment
Jeg vil gå til min leilighet

I can go with you to the bus station
Jeg kan gå med deg til busstasjonen

I need to leave the museum.
Jeg må forlate museet.

I like to eat oranges.
Jeg liker å spise appelsiner.

I like to take the train
Jeg liker å ta toget

I am going to teach a class
Jeg skal undervise en klasse

I have to speak to my teacher
Jeg trenger å snakke med min lærer

Please master *every* single page up until here prior to attempting the following two pages!

You want / do you want?
Du vil / vil du?
He wants / does he want?
Han vil / vil han?
She wants / does she want?
Hun vil / vil hun?
We want / do we want?
Vi vil / vil vi?
They want / do they want?
De vil / vil de?
(Plural) You want / do you want?
Dere vil / vil dere?

You need / do you need?
Du trenger / trenger du?
He needs / does he need?
Han trenger / trenger han?
She needs / does she need?
Hun trenger / trenger hun?
We need / do we need?
Vi trenger / trenger vi?
They need / do they need?
De trenger / trenger de?
(Plural) You need / do you need?
Dere trenger / trenger dere?

You can / can you?
Du kan / kan du?
He can / can he?
Han kan / kan han?
She can / can she?
Hun kan / kan hun?
We can / can we?
Vi kan / kan vi?
They can / can they?
De kan / Kan de?
(Plural) You can / can you?
Dere kan / kan dere

You like / do you like?
Du liker / liker du?
He likes / does he like?
Han liker / liker han?
She like / does she like?
Hun liker / liker hun?
We like / do we like?
Vi liker / liker vi?
They like / do they like?
De liker / liker du?
(Plural) You like / do you like?
Dere liker / liker dere?

You go / do you go?
Du går / går du?
He goes / does he go?
Han går / går han?
She goes / does she go?
Hun går / går hun?
We go / do we go?
Vi går / går vi?
They go / do they go?
De går / går de?
(Plural) You go / do you go?
Dere går / går dere?

You have / do you have?
Du har / har du?
He has / does he have?
Han har / har han?
She has / does she have?
Hun har / har hun?
We have / do we have?
Vi har / har vi?
They have / do they have?
De har / har de?
(Plural) You have / do you have?
Dere har / har dere?

Do you want to go?
Vil du gå?

Does he want to fly?
Vil han fly?

We want to swim
Vi vil svømme?

Do they want to run?
Vil de løpe?

Do you need to clean?
Trenger du å vaske?

She needs to sing a song
Hun trenger å synge en sang

We need to travel
Vi trenger å reise

They don't need to fight
De trenger ikke å krangle

You (plural) need to save your money.
Dere må spare pengene deres.

Can you hear me?
Kan du høre meg?

He can dance very well
Han kan danse veldig bra

We can go out tonight
Vi kan gå ut i kveld

The fireman can break the door during an emergency.
Brannmannen kan bryte opp døren under en nødsituasjon.

Do you like to eat here?
Liker du å spise her?

He likes to spend time here
Han liker å tilbringe tid her

We like to fix the house
Vi liker å fikse huset

They like to cook
De liker å lage mat
*"To cook" is translated as "to make food" = *å lage mat*.

You (plural) like to play soccer.
Dere liker å spille fotball.

Do you go to the movies on weekends? walk outside
Går du på kino i helgene? gå utenfor

He goes fishing
Han skal fiske

We are going to relax
Vi skal slappe av

They go out to eat at a restaurant everyday.
De går ut og spiser på en restaurant hver dag.

Do you have money?
Har du penger?

She must look outside
Hun må se ut

We have to sign our names
Vi trenger å signere våre navn

They have to send the letter
De trenger å sende brevet

You (plural) have to stand in line.
Dere må stå i kø.

Other Useful Tools in the Norwegian Language

Days of the Week
Sunday - Søndag
Monday - Mandag
Tuesday - Tirsdag
Wednesday - Onsdag
Thursday - Torsdag
Friday - Fredag
Saturday - Lørdag

Months
January - Januar
February - Februar
March - Mars
April - April
May - Mai
June - Juni
July - Juli
August - August
September - September
October - Oktober
November - November
December - Desember

Seasons
Spring - Vår
Summer - Sommer
Autumn - Høst
Winter - Vinter

Colors
Black - Svart
White - Hvit
Gray - Grå
Red - Rød
Blue - Blå
Yellow - Gul
Green - Grønn
Orange - Oransje
Purple - Lilla
Brown - Brun

Cardinal Directions
North Nord
South - Sør
East - Øst
West - Vest

Numbers
One - En
Two - To
Three - Tre
Four - Fire
Five - Fem
Six - Seks
Seven – Sju / sy
Eight - Åtte
Nine - Ni
Ten - Ti
Eleven – Elleve
Twelve – Tolv
Thirteen – Tretten
Fourteen – Fjorten
Fifteen – Femten
Sixteen – Seksten
Seventeen – Sytten
Eighteen – Atten
Nineteen – Nitten
Twenty – Tjue
Thirty – Tretti
Forty – Førti
Fifty – Femti
Sixty – Seksti
Seventy – Sytti
Eighty – Åtti
Ninety – Nitti
Hundred – Hundre
Thousand – Ett tusen
Million – Én million
Billion – Én milliard

Conversational Swedish Quick and Easy
The Most Innovative Technique to Learn the Swedish Language

YATIR NITZANY

The Swedish Language

Sweden is a northern European country of 10 million people. For various political and geographical reasons, immigration and emigration have played big parts in its language concerns. While in 1900, Sweden had a population of 5.1 million with the majority speaking Swedish, this has now doubled due to an influx of immigrants. The influx of immigrants has greatly increased the number of languages spoken in Sweden, particularly in institutional settings such as preschool and adult education.
There was no official Swedish language until 2009, when the "Swedish Language Act" was implemented, making Swedish the official language in the country.

However, minority groups in the north spoke Sami or Finnish. The country faced difficult times politically, economically, and religiously, which led to a significant number of emigrants to the US over the years. The estimate is that 10% of the population emigrated to the US.

The 2009 act had its roots in a nationalistic language policy from the 1880s, which aimed to promote the Swedish language and culture among minority groups. However, children in Sweden also have the right to mother-tongue tuition in compulsory school.

Swedish is a language of the East Scandinavian group of the Germanic branch of the Indo-European language family. It is spoken not only in Sweden, but also in countries such as Canada, Estonia, Finland, Norway, United Arab Emirates, and the United States. It is closely related to Norwegian and Danish and developed from Old Norse.

Swedish can be divided into three main dialect areas: Northern Swedish (Norrland), Eastern Swedish (Finland Swedish, Estonian Swedish), and Svea, Gutniska (Gutamal, Gotlandic, Gutnic). Standard Swedish is based on the Svea variety spoken in Stockholm, Uppsala, Lund, Gothenburg, and Helsinki, and is cultivated by the Svenska språknämnden, the official Swedish language board responsible for setting language standards.

About 11 million people worldwide speak Swedish, of which 10.5 million in Sweden itself.

Reading and Pronunciation in Swedish

Vowels

A – Hard vowel and pronounced like the "a" in "rather"

E – Soft vowel and pronounced like the the "e" in "fear"

I – Soft vowel and pronounced like the "ee" in "jeep"

O – Hard vowel and pronounced like the "o" in "crop" and the long "o" sounds like the "oo" in "cool"

U – Hard vowel and pronounced like the "u" in English but pronounced further back in the throat sounding like an "ew"

Y – Soft vowel and pronounced like the "ee" in "jeep"

Å – Hard vowel and pronounced like the "o" in "core"

Ä – Soft vowel and pronounced like the "ai" in "fair"

Ö – Soft vowel and pronounced like the "er" in "her"

Consonants

G – preceding a hard vowel A, O, U and Å is pronounced as G

G – preceding a soft vowel E, I, Y, Ä or Ö is pronounced as "y" as in "yell"

G – when proceeding an L or an R is pronounced as G

NG – pronounced as "ng" as in "young"

GN – sounds like a "ng" however immediately followed by another "n"

J – When it's placed as the first letter of a word its pronounced as a "y"

SJ – is pronounced like "h" as in "ham". However, that "h" is pronounced further back in the throat

TJ – pronounced as "sh" as in "shirt"

GJ, LJ, DJ, and HJ – all pronounced as "y"

K – when preceding a consonant then it's pronounced as "k"

K – when preceding a E, I, Y, Ä or Ö and J, it is pronounced as "sh" as in "shirt"

SK – when preceding a hard vowel, it's pronounced as "sk" as in "skull"

SK – when preceding a soft vowel, it is pronounced like "h" as in "hat." However, that "h" is pronounced further back in your throat

RS – is pronounced as "sh" in English "shell"

Words ending in *sion* or *tion* are also pronounced as that "h."

The Program

I am - Jag är
With you - Med dig
With him / with her - Med honom / med henne
With us - Hos/med oss
For you - För/till dig
Without him - Utan honom
Without them - Utan dem
Always - Alltid
At the (or**) In** - Vid
This (or**) this is** - Detta / detta är
You, you are - Du, du är
Sometimes - Ibland
Maybe - Kanske
Are you - Är du
With - Med
Today - Idag
He (or**) he is** - Han / han är
She (or**) she is** - Hon / hon är
From - Från

Sentences from the vocabulary (now you can speak the sentences and connect the words)

I am with you.
Jag är med dig.
I am always with her.
Jag är alltid med henne.
I am from Sweden.
Jag är från Sverige.
This is for you.
Det här är till dig.
Are you from Stockholm?
Är du från Stockholm?
Are you at the house?
Är du vid huset?
Sometimes I go without him.
Ibland går jag utan honom.
Are you alone today?
Är du ensam idag?

I was - Jag var
To be - Att vara
Good - Bra
Better - Bättre
Preferable - Att föredra
And - Och
Very - Mycket
Between - Mellan
Now - Nu
Happy - Glad
Later - Senare
If - Om
Yes - Ja
Then - Sedan
Tomorrow - Imorgon
Here - Här
Also / too / as well - Också
Also / too / as well - Likaså

I was home at 5pm.
Jag var hemma vid 17.

Between now and tomorrow.
Mellan nu och imorgon

It's better to be home later.
Det är bättre att vara hemma senare.

If this is good, then I am happy.
Om det här är bra så är jag glad.

Yes, you are very good.
Ja, du är väldigt bra.

I was here with them.
Jag var här med dem.

You and I.
Du och jag.

The - Den
Same - Samma
After - Efter
Ok - Ok
Even if - Även om
Afterwards – Efteråt
Worse - Värre
Where - Var
Everything - Allt
Anything - Vad som helst
Somewhere - Någonstans
What - Vad
Almost - Nästan
There - Där

Afterwards is worse.
Efteråt är det värre.

Even if I go now.
Även om jag går nu.

Where is everything?
Var är allt?

Maybe somewhere.
Kanske någonstans.

What? I am almost there.
Vad? Jag är nästan där.

Where are you?
Var är du?

This is for us.
Det här är för oss.

The same day.
Samma dag.

*This *isn't* a phrase book! The purpose of this book is *solely* to provide you with the tools to create *your own* sentences!

Thank you - Tack
House - Hus
Still - Fortfarande
Car - Bil
Already - Redan
Good morning - God morgon
How are you - Hur mår du
But / However - Men / Dock
Hello - Hej
What is your name - Vad heter du
How old are you - Hur gammal är du
Son - Son
Daughter - Dotter
Impossible - Omöjligt
Hard - Hårt
Without us - Utan oss

She is not in the car, so maybe she is still at the house?
Hon är inte i bilen, så hon kanske är hemma fortfarande?

I am in the car already with your son and daughter.
Jag sitter redan i bilen med din son och dotter.

Good morning, how are you today?
God morgon, hur mår du idag?

Hello, what is your name?
Hej, vad heter du?

How old are you?
Hur gammal är du?

This is very hard, but it's not impossible.
Det här är väldigt svårt, men det är inte omöjligt.

Where are you from?
Var kommer du ifrån?

Thank you, Alexander.
Tack, Alexander.

For - För
To go - Att gå
It is - Det är
Time - Tid
Without - Utan
No / not - Nej / inte
Late - Sen
Away - Borta
That (or) **that is** - Det / det är
Similar - Liknande
Other - Andra
Side - Side
Until - Tills
Yesterday - Igår
Almost - Nästan
Since - Sedan
Day - Dag
Before - Förr

It is almost time to go.
Det är snart dags att gå.
I am not here, I am away.
Jag är inte här, jag är borta.
That house is similar to ours.
Det huset liknar vårt.
I am from the other side.
Jag är från andra sidan.
But I was here until late yesterday.
Men jag var här till sent igår.
The coffee is without sugar.
Kaffet är utan socker.

*In Swedish there are three definitions for the word "time": *gånger*, *tid* and *klockan*
"How many times?" - *Hur många **gånger**?*
"During the time of the dinosaurs." - *Under dinosauriernas **tid**.*
"What time is it?" - *Vad är **klockan**?*
* However, you may say: "What time should we meet?" *Vilken tid ska vi träffas?* Since in Swedish, we say "What is the clock?" instead of "what time is it?"

I say / I am saying - Jag säger
Happy - Happy
I want - Jag vill (ha)
Without you - Utan dig
Everywhere - Överallt
I go / I am going - Jag går
To - Till
My - Min
Cousin - Kusin
I need - Jag behöver
Idea - Idé
Night - Natt
To see - Att se
Light - Ljus
Outside - Utanför
That - Att/det
That he is - att han är
That she is - Att hon är
I see / I am seeing - Jag ser

I am saying no!
Jag säger nej!
I want to see this in the day.
Jag vill se detta på dagen.
I see this everywhere.
Jag ser detta överallt.
I am happy to be here without my cousin.
Jag är glad att vara här utan min kusin.
I need to be there at night.
Jag måste vara där på natten.
You need to be at home.
Du måste vara hemma.
I am seeing light outside.
Jag ser ljus utanför.
I need to know that that is a good idea.
Jag måste veta att det är en bra idé.
What time is it right now?
Vad är klockan just nu?

Place - Plats
Easy - Lätt
To find - Att hitta
To look - Att leta / titta
To look for - Att leta efter
To search - Att söka
Near – Nära, i närheten
To wait - Att vänta
To sell - Att sälja
To use - Att använda
To know - Att veta
To decide - Att bestämma
Between - Mellan
Two - Två
Both - Båda
I can – Jag kan / **Can I?** – Kan jag?

This place is easy to find.
Denna plats är lätt att hitta.
I am saying to wait until tomorrow.
Jag säger att vi väntar tills imorgon.
Is it easy to sell this table?
Är det lätt att sälja det här bordet?
I want to use this.
Jag vill använda den här.
I want to know where is the grocery store.
Jag vill veta var mataffären är.
I need to decide between both places.
Jag måste välja mellan båda ställena.
Is it possible to look for this book in the library?
Kan man leta efter den här boken på biblioteket?
I am very happy to know that everything is ok.
Jag är väldigt glad över att veta att allt är ok.
Is this place near?
Är det här stället nära?
I can work today.
Jag kan jobba idag.
I do what I want.
Jag gör vad jag vill.

Because - Eftersom
Much, many, a lot - Mycket, många, mycket
Both - Båda
Them / They - De
Their - Deras
Book - Bok
Mine - Min
To understand - **Att** förstå
Problem / problems - Problem
There are/ there is - Det finns
To buy – Att köpa
Like this - Så här
View - Utsikt
Food - Mat
Water - Vatten
Hotel - Hotell
Many - Många / **Much / a lot** - Mycket
A little – Lite
I do / I am doing - Jag gör

I like this hotel because it's near the beach.
Jag gillar det här hotellet eftersom det är nära stranden.
I want to look at the view.
Jag vill titta på utsikten.
I want to buy a water bottle.
Jag vill köpa en vattenflaska.
Do it like this!
Gör så här!
There are many tourists in Sweden, Denmark, Norway and Finland every summer.
Det är många turister i Sverige, Danmark, Norge och Finland varje sommar.
That book is mine.
Den boken är min. / Det där är min bok.
I have to understand the problem.
Jag måste förstå problemet.
I see the view of the city from my hotel room.
Jag ser utsikten över staden från mitt hotellrum.

I like - Jag gillar
I enjoy - Jag njuter (av)
Of - Av
Parents - Föräldrar
Why - Varför
To say - **Att** säga
Good morning - God morgon
I will be - Jag kommer att vara
Ready - Klar
Ready - Färdig
Soon - Snart
Quickly - Snabbt
To work - Att jobba
Who - Vem
Something - Något
Important - Viktigt
Busy - Upptagen

I like to be at my house with my parents.
Jag gillar att vara hemma med mina föräldrar.

Why do I need to say something important?
Varför behöver jag säga något viktigt?

I am there with him.
Jag är där med honom.

I am busy, but I will be ready quickly.
Jag är upptagen, men jag kommer att vara färdig snabbt.

I like to work.
Jag gillar att arbeta.

Who is there?
Vem är där?

I want to know if they are here.
Jag vill veta om de är här.

I can go outside.
Jag kan gå ut.

There is a taxi outside.
Det finns en taxi utanför.

How much - Hur mycket
To bring - **Att** ta med
With me - Med mig
Instead - Istället
Only - Endast
When - När
Do I - Gör jag
Money - Pengar
Were - Var
Without me - Utan mig
Fast - Snabb
Slow - Långsam
Cold - Kallt
Inside - Inuti
To eat - Att äta
Hot - Hot
To Drive - Att köra
Can you – Kan du
Lunch – Lunch

How much money do I need to bring with me?
Hur mycket pengar behöver jag ta med mig?
I like bread instead of rice.
Jag skulle vilja ha bröd istället för ris.
Only when you can.
Bara när du kan.
Go there without me.
Gå dit utan mig.
I need to drive in the car very fast or very slow.
Jag måste köra bilen väldigt fort eller väldigt långsamt.
It is already there.
Den finns redan där.
Is it cold at the library?
Är det kallt på biblioteket?
I like to eat a hot meal for my lunch.
Jag gillar att äta en varm måltid till lunch.
This is a good meal.
Det här är en god måltid.

To answer – Att svara
To fly – Att flyga
To travel – Att resa
To learn - Att lära
How - Hur
To swim - Att simma
To practice - Att träna
To play - Att spela
To leave - Att lämna
To come - Att komma
Our - Vår
Pool - Pool
First - Först
Time - Tid

I need to answer many questions.
Jag behöver svara på många frågor.

I want to fly today.
Jag vill flyga idag.

I need to learn how to swim at our pool.
Jag måste lära mig att simma i vår pool.

I want to learn how to play better tennis.
Jag vill lära mig att spela tennis bättre.

I want to leave my dog at home.
Jag vill lämna min hund hemma.

I want to travel the world.
Jag vill resa jorden runt.

Since the first time.
Sedan första gången.

The children are yours!
Barnen är dina!

Come here quickly.
Kom hit snabbt.

Nobody - Ingen
Anyone - Någon
Against - Mot
Us - Oss
we – Vi
We are - Vi är
To visit - Att besöka
Mom - Mamma
To give - Att ge
Around - Runt
Week - Vecka
To meet - Att träffa
Someone - Någon
Just - Bara
To walk - Att gå
You *(indirect object)* - Dig
Nothing - Ingenting
Family - Familj
Each / Every - Varje

Something is better than nothing.
Något är bättre än inget.
I am against.
Jag är emot.
We go to visit my family each week.
Vi besöker min familj varje vecka.
I need to give you something.
Jag måste ge dig något.
Do you want to meet someone?
Vill du träffa någon?
I am here tomorrow as well.
Jag är här imorgon också.
You do this every day?
Gör du detta varje dag?
You need to walk around the school.
Du måste gå runt i skolan.

Dig is the indirect object pronoun of the pronoun "you," the person who is actually affected by the action that is being carried out.

I have - Jag har
To look like - Att se ut som
Like (preposition) - Som
Friend - Vän
To borrow - Att låna
On - På
About - Om
Grandfather - Farfar
Grandfather - Morfar
To want – att vilja
To stay - Att stanna
To continue - Att fortsätta
Way - Väg
That's why - Det är därför
To show - Att visa
To prepare - Att förbereda
I don't have - Jag har inte
Breakfast - Frukost
Man - Man

Do you want to look like a Joshua?
Vill du se ut som en Joshua?

I want to borrow this book for my grandfather.
Jag vill låna den här boken till min farfar.

I want to drive and to continue on this way to my house.
Jag vill köra och fortsätta på den här vägen hem till mig.

I want to stay in Gothenburg because I have a friend there.
Jag vill stanna i Göteborg eftersom jag har en kompis där.

I need to show you how to prepare breakfast.
Jag måste visa dig hur man lagar frukost.

Why don't you have the book?
Varför har du inte boken?

I don't need the car today.
Jag behöver inte bilen idag.

Our house is located on the mountain.
Vårt hus ligger på berget.

To remember - Att komma ihåg
Your - Din/ditt
Number - Nummer
Hour - Timme
Darkness - Mörker
To speak / to talk - Att tala / prata
Grandmother – Mormor/farmor
Five - Fem
Minute / minutes - Minut / minuter
More - Mer
To think - Att tänka
To do - Att göra
To come - Att komma
To hear - Att höra
Last - Sista
To call - Att ringa
Brother - Bror
Dad - Pappa

I want to call my brother and my dad today.
Jag vill ringa min bror och min pappa idag.

You need to remember your number.
Du måste komma ihåg ditt nummer.

This is the last hour of darkness.
Detta är mörkrets sista timme.

I want to come with you.
Jag vill följa med dig.

I can hear my grandmother speaking Swedish.
Jag kan höra min mormor prata svenska.

I need to think about this more.
Jag måste tänka mer på detta.

From here to there, it's just five minutes.
Härifrån till dit är det bara fem minuter.

*With the knowledge you've gained so far, now try to create your own sentences!

To leave - Att lämna
Again - Återigen
Again - Igen
Early - Tidigt
To take - Att ta
To try - Att prova
To rent – Att hyra
Without her - Utan henne
Beach - Strand
To turn off - Att stänga av
To ask – Att fråga, be om
To stop - Att stanna
Permission - Tillstånd
Different - Annorlunda
Man - Man
See you soon - Vi ses snart
Goodbye - Hejdå

I need to rent a house on the beach.
Jag behöver hyra ett hus vid stranden.

I want to take this with me.
Jag vill ta det här med mig.

We want to stop here.
Vi vill stanna här.

I need to turn off the lights early.
Jag måste släcka ljuset tidigt

We are from Scandinavia.
Vi är från Skandinavien.

Your doctor is in the same building.
Din läkare är i samma byggnad.

In order to leave you have to ask permission.
För att kunna lämna måste du be om tillstånd.

He is a different man now.
Han är en annan man nu.

Goodbye my friend.
Adjö, min vän.

To open - Att öppna
Sad - Ledsen
Without - Utan
Sister - Syster
To hope - Att hoppas
To live - Att leva
Nice to meet you - Trevligt att träffa dig
Name - Namn
Last name - Efternamn
To return – (För) Att återvända
Enough - Nog
Door - Dörr

I need to open the door for my sister.
Jag måste öppna dörren för min syster.

I need to buy something.
Jag måste köpa något.

I want to meet your brothers.
Jag vill träffa dina bröder.

Nice to meet you. What is your name and your last name?
Trevligt att träffas. Vad är ditt för-och-efternamn?

We can hope for a better future.
Vi kan hoppas på en bättre framtid.

It is impossible to live without problems.
Det är omöjligt att leva utan problem.

I want to return to the United States.
Jag vill återvända till USA.

Why are you sad right now?
Varför är du ledsen just nu?

I want to go to sleep.
Jag vill gå och lägga mig.

Where is the airport?
Var är flygplatsen?

*This *isn't* a phrase book! The purpose of this book is *solely* to provide you with the tools to create *your own* sentences!

To happen - Att hända
To order - Att beställa
To drink - Att dricka
To keep - Att behålla
Child - Barn
Woman - Kvinna
To begin - Att börja
To finish - Att avsluta
To help - Att hjälpa
To smoke - Att röka
To love - Att älska
To like - Att tycka om
Excuse me - Ursäkta mig
Sorry - Förlåt
Swedish - Svenska

This needs to happen today.
Detta måste hända idag.
My child he is here as well.
Mitt barn, han är här också.
I want to order a soup.
Jag vill beställa en soppa.
We want to start the class soon.
Vi vill börja lektionen snart.
In order to finish at three o'clock this afternoon, I need to finish soon.
För att avsluta vid tretiden i eftermiddag måste jag bli klar snart
I want to learn how to speak Swedish perfectly.
Jag vill lära mig att prata perfekt svenska.
I don't want to smoke again.
Jag vill inte röka igen.
I want to help.
Jag vill hjälpa till.
I love you.
Jag älskar dig.
I see you.
Jag ser dig.
I need you.
Jag behöver dig.

Dig is the direct object pronoun of the pronoun "you."

To read - Att läsa
To write - Att skriva
To teach - Att undervisa
To close - Att stänga
To turn on - Att tända
To prefer - Att föredra
To put – att lägga
Less - Mindre
Sun - Sol
Month - Månad
I talk - Jag pratar
Exact – Exakt
Date – Datum
Possible – Möjlig
In order to - För att
For me – För/till mig

I need this book to learn how to read and write in Swedish.
Jag behöver den här boken för att lära mig läsa och skriva på svenska.
I want to teach English in Sweden.
Jag vill undervisa i engelska i Sverige.
I want turn on the lights and close the door.
Jag vill tända ljuset och stänga dörren.
I want to pay less than you.
Jag vill betala mindre än dig.
I prefer to put this here.
Jag föredrar att lägga detta här.
I talk with the boy and with the girl in Swedish.
Jag pratar med pojken och med tjejen på svenska.
I need to go outside.
Jag måste gå ut.
Is it possible to know the exact date of the flight?
Är det möjligt att veta det exakta datumet för flyget?
Is this for me?
Är det här för/till mig?
I want to go to sleep now because I need to wake up early in order to take a taxi to the airport.
Jag vill gå och lägga mig nu för jag måste vakna tidigt för att ta en taxi till flygplatsen.

To exchange - Att växla
To sit - Att sitta
Together - Tillsammans
To change - Att ändra
Of course - Naturligtvis
Welcome - Välkommen
To arrive - Att anlända
Years - År
Sky - himmel
Up - Upp
Down - Ner
Below, under – Nedan, under
Sorry - Förlåt
To follow - Att följa
Theater - Teater
Big - Stor
New – Ny, nytt
Never - Aldrig

Of course I can come to the theater, and I want to sit together with you and your family.
Självklart kan jag komma till teatern, och jag vill sitta tillsammans med dig och din familj.
I can see the sky from the window.
Jag kan se himlen från fönstret.
I want to exchange the money at the bank.
Jag vill växla pengarna på banken.
If you look under the table, you can see the new rug.
Om du tittar under bordet kan du se den nya mattan.
I am sorry.
Jag är ledsen.
The dog wants to follow me to the store.
Hunden vill följa mig till affären.
I don't ever want to see you.
Jag vill aldrig se dig.

*In Swedish "to call (on the phone)" is *ringa*. However, to call out to someone is *kallade*.

To allow - Att tillåta
To believe - Att tro
Kitchen - Kök
Except - Förutom
To promise - Att lova
Good night - God natt
To recognize - Att känna igen
People - Människor
To move - Att flytta
Far - Långt
Kitchen - Kök
To enter - att komma in
To receive - Att ta emot
Throughout – Genomgående / genom
Good afternoon - God eftermiddag
Through - Genom
Him - Honom
Her - henne

I need to believe everything except for this.
Jag måste tro på allt utom detta.
I must promise myself not to forget to say good night to my parents each night.
Jag måste lova mig själv att inte glömma att säga godnatt till mina föräldrar varje kväll.
I need to allow him to go with us.
Jag måste tillåta honom att följa med oss.
I can't recognize him.
Jag kan inte känna igen honom.
I need to move my car because my sister needs to move her things to her car
Jag behöver flytta min bil eftersom min syster behöver flytta sina saker till sin bil.
I see the sun from the kitchen window throughout the morning.
Jag ser solen från köksfönstret hela morgonen.
I go into the house from the front entrance and not through the yard.
Jag går in i huset från den främre entrén och inte genom gården.

To wish - **Att** önska
Bad - Dåligt
To get - Att få
To forget - Att glömma
Everybody - Alla
Although - Fast
To feel - Att känna
Good - Bra
Next (following/after) – Näst/härnäst
Next to (near/close) – Nära / bredvid
I must - Jag måste
In front - Framför
Person - Person
Behind - Bakom
Which - Vilken
Restaurant - Restaurang
Bathroom - Badrum

I don't want to wish you anything bad.
Jag vill inte önska dig något ont.
I must forget everybody from my past.
Jag måste glömma alla från mitt förflutna.
To feel well I must take vitamins.
För att må bra måste jag ta vitaminer.
I am near the person that's behind you.
Jag är nära personen som är bakom dig.
Which is the best restaurant in the area?
Vilken är den bästa restaurangen i området?
I can feel the heat.
Jag kan känna värmen.
She must get a car before the next year.
Hon måste skaffa en bil innan nästa år.
I need to repair a part of the cabinet in the bathroom.
Jag behöver laga en del av skåpet i badrummet.

*In the Swedish language the word "next" has two definitions *nästa* and *bredvid*.
- "The next day" - *nästa dag*.
- "Next to me" - *bredvid mig*.

Please - Snälla
Beautiful - Vackert
To lift - Att lyfta
Include / Including - Inkludera
Belong - Tillhör
To hold - Att hålla
To check - Att kolla
Small - Liten
Real - Riktig
Even though - Trots att
Thing - Sak
Doesn't - Gör det inte
So (as in *then*) - Så
So (as in *so much / so many*) - Så
Price - Pris

This week the weather was very beautiful.
Den här veckan var vädret väldigt vackert.
Is that a real diamond?
Är det där en riktig diamant?
I want to lift this.
Jag vill lyfta det här.
The sun is high in the sky.
Solen står högt på himlen.
Can you please put the wood in the fire?
Kan du snälla lägga veden i elden?
Can you please hold my hand?
Kan du vara snäll och hålla min hand?
We need to check the size of the house.
Vi måste kolla storleken på huset.
I can pay this although the price is expensive.
Jag kan betala detta även om priset är dyrt.
Does the price include everything?
Är allt inkluderat i priset?
So why is this so small?
Så varför är detta så litet?

*In the Swedish lanugage the word "so" has two definitions; "So, where are you?" - så, var är du? "There are so many." - det finns så många.

Building Bridges

In Building Bridges, we take six conjugated verbs that have been selected after studies I have conducted for several months in order to determine which verbs are most commonly conjugated, and which are then automatically followed by an infinitive verb. For example, once you know how to say, "I need," "I want," "I can," and "I like," you will be able to connect words and say almost anything you want more correctly and understandably. The following three pages contain these six conjugated verbs in first, second, third, fourth, and fifth person, as well as some sample sentences. Please master the entire program up until *here* prior to venturing onto this section.

I Can - Jag kan
I Do - Jag gör
I go - Jag går
I need - Jag behöver
I want - Jag vill ha
I see - Jag ser
I Like - Jag gillar
I say - Jag säger
I talk - Jag pratar
I have – Jag har
I have to / I must – Jag behöver / Jag måste

I want to go home.
Jag vill gå hem.
I need to find a hospital.
Jag behöver hitta ett sjukhus.
I need to walk outside the museum.
Jag behöver gå utanför museet.
I like to eat oranges.
Jag gillar att äta apelsiner.
I can go with you.
Jag kan gå med dig.
I am seeing a house today.
Jag ska titta på/se ett hus idag.
I am talking with you.
Jag pratar med dig.

Please master *every* single page up until here prior to attempting the following two pages!

You want / do you want?
Du vill / vill du?
He wants / does he want?
Han vill/vill han?
She wants / does she want?
Hon vill/vill hon?
We want / do we want?
Vi vill / vill vi?
They want / do they want?
De vill / vill de?
You (Plural) want/ do you (Pl) want?
Ni vill / Vill ni?

You need / do you need?
Du behöver / behöver du?
He needs / does he need?
Han behöver/behöver han?
She needs / does she need?
Hon behöver/behöver hon?
We need / do we need?
Vi behöver / behöver vi?
They need / do they need?
De behöver / behöver de?
You (Pl)need/ do you (Pl) need?
Ni behöver / Behöver ni?

You can / can you?
Du kan/kan du?
He can / can he?
Han kan/kan han?
She can / can she?
Hon kan/kan hon?
We can / can we?
Vi kan/kan vi?
They can / can they?
De kan/kan de?
You (Pl) can/ can you?
Ni kan / Kan ni?

You do / do you do?
Du gör/gör du?
He does / does he do?
Han gör/gör han?
She does / does she do?
Hon gör/gör hon?
We do / do we do?
Vi gör / gör vi?
They do / do they do?
De gör / gör de?
You (Pl) do/ do you (Pl) do?
Ni gör / Gör ni?

You go / do you go?
Du går / går du?
He goes / does he go?
Han går / går han?
She goes / does she go?
Hon går / går hon?
We go / do we go?
Vi går / går vi?
They go / do they go?
De går / går de?
You (Pl) go/ do you (Pl) go?
Ni går / Går ni?

You must / do you have to?
Du måste/måste du?
He must / does he have to?
Han måste/måste han?
She must / does she have to?
Hon måste/måste hon?
We must / do we have to?
Vi måste/måste vi?
They must / do they have to?
De måste/måste de?
You (Pl) must/ do you have to?
Ni måste / Måste ni?

Do you want to go?
Vill du gå?

Does he want to fly?
Vill han flyga?

She wants to go to the bus station.
Hon vill gå till busstationen.

We want to swim.
Vi vill simma.

Do they want to run?
Vill de springa?

Do you need to clean?
Behöver du städa?

She needs to sing a song.
Hon måste sjunga en sång.

We need to travel.
Vi behöver resa.

They don't need to fight.
De behöver inte slåss.

You (plural) need to save your money.
Ni (plural) behöver spara era pengar.

Can you hear me?
Kan du höra mig?

He can dance very well.
Han kan dansa väldigt bra.

We can go out tonight.
Vi kan gå ut ikväll.

The fireman can break the door during an emergency.
Brandmannen kan slå in dörren under en nödsituation.

Do you like to eat here?
Gillar du att äta här?

We like to stay in the house.
Vi gillar att bo i huset.

They like to cook.
De gillar att laga mat.

You (plural) like to play soccer.
Ni (plural) gillar att spela fotboll.

Do you go to the movies on weekends?
Går du på bio på helgerna?

He goes /fishing.
Han går och fiskar.

They go out to eat at a restaurant every day.
De går ut och äter på en restaurang varje dag.

Do you have money?
Har du pengar?

She must look outside.
Hon måste titta utanför.

They have to send the letter.
De måste skicka brevet.

You (plural) have to stand in line.
Ni (plural) måste stå i kö.

Other Useful Tools in the Swedish Language

Numbers - Siffror
One - Ett
Two - Två
Three - Tre
Four - Fyra
Five - Fem
Six - Sex
Seven - Sju
Eight - Åtta
Nine - Nio
Ten - Tio

Days of the Week - Veckodagar
Sunday - Söndag
Monday - Måndag
Tuesday - Tisdag
Wednesday - Onsdag
Thursday - Torsdag
Friday - Fredag
Saturday - Lördag

Seasons - Årstider
Spring - Vår/ **Summer** - Sommar
Autumn - Höst / **Winter** - Vinter

Colors - Färger
Black - Svart
White - Vit
Gray – Grå
Red - Röd
Blue - Blå
Yellow - Gul
Green - Grön
Orange - Orange
Purple - Lila
Brown - Brun

Cardinal Directions - Väderstreck
North - Norr/**South** - Söder
East - Öster/ **West** - Väster

Conversational Yiddish Quick and Easy
The Most Innovative Technique to Learn the Yiddish Language

YATIR NITZANY

The Yiddish Language

Written with Hebrew alphabet characters, Yiddish is a High German language that was used by Jews from central and Eastern Europe before the Holocaust. Most likely beginning around the ninth century CE, Yiddish was developed over the course of several centuries by Ashkenazi Jews in the Holy Roman Empire. Yiddish combined a Germanic language base with some Aramaic, Hebrew, Slavic, and even a smattering of Romance language words to create a distinct patois that served to unite diverse Jewish populations in Europe following the Diaspora. As Jewish communities grew in Europe, the Yiddish language grew with them, eventually including as many as ten to thirteen million speakers. However, the deaths of six million Jews in the Holocaust and the subsequent dispersal of Jewish communities following World War II decimated the ranks of Yiddish speakers in the twentieth century, and currently, it is estimated that as few as two million people worldwide still speak Yiddish. Nonetheless, some Yiddish words have been absorbed by many of the languages with which Yiddish cultures interacted following World War II (including chutzpah, glitch, kitsch, klutz, kosher, schtum, schmooze, and verklempt, among others, in English). Today, the language is enjoying a resurgence in Hasidic Jewish communities where it is the primary language spoken.

The Program

Memorize the vocabulary:

I - E'ech איך
I am - E'ech bin איך בין
With you - Mit deer מיט דיר
With us - Mit untz מיט אונז
For you - Far deir פאר דיר
For you - *(formal)* Far ir פאר איר
Are you? Du bist? ?דו ביסט
You are - Bistu ביסטו
You - Du, דו
You - Di די
You - *(formal)* Ir איר
You - *(plural)* Alle אלע
From - Fin (galitziana) פין
From - Foon (litvak) פון

Sentences composed from the vocabulary you just learned.

I am from Germany
E'ech bin fin Deuchland
איך בין פון דייטשלאנד

Are you from Israel?
Du bist fun Yisroel?
?דו ביסט פון ישׂראל

I am with you
E'ech bin mit dier
איך בין מיט דיר

This is for you.
Duce iz far dier
דאס איז פאר דיר

*This isn't a phrase book! The purpose of this book is *solely* to provide you with the tools to create *your own* sentences!

With him - Mit eim מיט אים
With her - Mit eer מיט איר
Without him - Oon aim אן אים
Without them - Nisht mit zai נישט מיט זיי
Always - Shten'dik שטענדיק
This - Duce דאס
This is - Dus iz דאס איז
Is - Iz איז
It's - Es iz עס איז
Is it? - Iz es?? איז עס??
Sometimes – Am'oole אמאל
You are - Bistu ביסטו
Are you? - Du bist?? דו ביסט??
He - Er ער
She - Zi זי
Today – Haynt היינט

Are you at the house?
Bistu in shtub?
ביסטו אין שטוב?

I am always with her.
E'ech bin shten'dik mit eer
איך בין שטענדיק מיט איר

Are you alone today?
bistu heynt aleyn?
ביסטו היינט אליין?

Sometimes I go without him.
A mol gey ikh on im.
אַ מאָל גיי איך אָן אים.

Nisht mit literally means "not with."

Was - Gev'ain געווען
Was - Iz gev'ain איז געווען
I was - E'ech bin gev'ain איך בין געווען
To be - Tsu zain צו זיין
Good – Goot גוט
Here – Do דא
Very – Zeyer זייער
And – Un און
Between – Tsvishn צווישן
If – Oi'bb אויב
Now – Yetst יעצט
Tomorrow – Morgen מארגן
Where are you from? - Fin vi bista? פון ווי ביסטו?
How old are you? - Vi alt bistu? ווי אלט ביסטו?

I was here with them
E'ech bein gev'ain do mit zei
איך בין געווען דא מיט זיי

You and I
Di un e'ech
די און איך

I was home at 5pm
ikh bin geven in der heym 5:00
איך בין געווען אין דער היים 5:00

Between now and tomorrow.
Tsvishn itst aun morgn.
צווישן איצט און מארגן.

Where are you from?
Fuhn vanet bistu?
פון וואנעט ביסטו?

How old are you?
Vi alt bistu?
ווי אלט ביסטו?

The – Di די
A - Ein אן
A - A א
Later - Shpeter שפעטער
After - Noch נאך
Afterwards – Nochdem נאכדעם
Yes – Yo יא
To – Tsu צו
Person - Mentsh מענטש
Happy – Gliklech גליקלעך
Happy – Tsufridn צופרידן
Better – Besser בעסער
Day – Toog טאג
Tomorrow – Morgen מארגן
Then – Demolt דעמאלט
Good morning - Gutt Morgen גוט מארגן
How are you? - Vas machstu? וואס מאכסטו?
Today – Haynt היינט

It's better to be home later.
Es iz beser tsu kumen aheym shpet.
עס איז בעסער צו קומען אהיים שפעטער.

If this is good, then I am happy.
oyb dos iz gut, bin ikh tsufridn.
אויב דאָס איז גוט, בין איך צופרידן.

Yes, you are very good
Yo, di bist zeyer git
יאָ, די ביסט זייער גיט

The same day
Di zelbe toog
די זעלבע טאג

Good morning, how are you today?
Gut morgn, vas machstu haynt?
גוט מארגן וואס מאכסטו היינט?

Where - Vu וואו
Where - Vi ווי
Ok – Okay אקאי
Everything - Alles אלעס
Everything - Alts אלץ
Somewhere – Ergets ערגעץ
Maybe - Efsher אפשר
What - Vus? וואס?
Almost – Shir nisht שיר נישט
There – Dort דארט
I go - E'ech gei איך גיי
Worse - Erger ערגער
Even if - Afil'e אפילו
No - Nein ניין

This is for us.
dos iz far undz.
דאָס איז פֿאַר אונדז.

Even if I go now
Afil'e oi'b e'ech gei yetst
אפילו אויב איך גיי יעצט

What? I am almost there
Vus? Eech bin bald dort
וואס? איך בין באלד דארט

Where are you?
Vu bist du?
ווי ביסטו?

Where is everything?
Vi iz alles?
ווי איז אלעס

Maybe somewhere
Efsher ergets
אפשר ערגעץ

Already – Shoin שוין
Son – Zun זון
Daughter – Tochter טאכטער
To have - Tsu hoben צו האבן
Doesn't - Nisht נישט
Hard - Shver שווער
Easy - Lae'echt לייכט
Still – Doch דאך
Impossible - Aummeglekh אוממעגלעך
House - Hoyz הויז
House - shteeb שטיב
Home - Haym היים
In, at, at the, in the - In אין
In, at, at the, in the - Baiביי
Car - Vugen וואגן
Car - Auto אויטא
Car - Mashin מאשין
Book - Buch בוך
He is - Er iz ער איז
She is - Zi iz זי איז
Isn't – Iz nisht איז נישט

She is not in the car, so maybe she is still at the house?
zi iz nit in oyto, iz efsher iz zi nokh in hoyz
?זי איז ניט אין אויטאָ, איז אפֿשר איז זי נאָך אין הויז

I am already in the car with your son and your daughter
E'ech bein shoiin in auto mit deyn zun aun deyn tochter
איך בין שוין אין אויטא מיט דיין זין און דיין טאכטער

This is very hard, but it's not impossible
Dos iz zeyer shver, ober es iz nisht aummeglekh
דאָס איז זייער שווער, אָבער עס איז נישט אוממעגלעך

Thank you – A sheinem dank א שיינעם דאנק
Thanks – A dank א דאנק
For – Far פאר
Anything – Alles אלעס
That - Duce דאס
That is - Duce iz דאס איז
But/however - Ober אבער
No - Nein ניין
Not - Nisht נישט
I am not - E'ech bin nisht איך בין נישט
Away – Avek אוועק
Same / like *(as in similar)* – Zelbe זעלבע
Like (preposition) – Vi ווי

Thank you, David.
A dank, Dovid.
א. דאַנק, דוד.

It's almost time
Ez iz shi'er der tsa'yt
עס איז שיער דער צייט

I am not here, I am far away
ikh bin nisht do, ikh bin vayt avek
איך בין נישט דאָ, איך בין ווייַט אוועק

That house is similar to ours.
dos hoyz iz enlekh tsu unzers.
דאָס הויז איז ענלעך צו אונדזערס.

*In Yiddish there are 3 definitions for "time":
Time - Tsa'yt צייט (reference to; hour, "what time is it?")
Time - Tseyt צייט (era, moment period, duration of time)
Time – Mol מאל (occasion or frequency)

*This *isn't* a phrase book! The purpose of this book is *solely* to provide you with the tools to create *your own* sentences!

I say / I am saying - E'ech zoog איך זאג
What time is it? - Vos iz der tsa'yt װאס איז דער צײט
I want - E'ech vil איך װיל
Without you - Oo'n dir אן דיר
Everywhere /wherever – Uberall איבעראל
I am going - E'ech gey איך גײ
With – Mit מיט
My – Mein מײן
Light - Le'echt לײכט
I need - E'ech darf איך דארף
I see / I am seeing - E'ech zei איך זע
Right now - Yetst יעצט

I am saying no / I say no
E'ech zoog az nisht
איך זאג אז נישט

You need to be at home.
Du darfst zayn in shtub.
דו דארפסט זײן אין שטוב

I see light outside
E'ech zei le'echt in draussen
איך זע ליכט אין דרויסן

What time is it right now?
Vos iz du tsa'yt yetst?
װאס איז די צײט יעצט?

I see this everywhere
E'ech zei duce uberall
איך זע דאס איבעראל

I want this car
E'ech vil duce mashin
איך װיל דאס מאשין

To see – Tzu zein צו זעהן
Outside - Droissen דרויסן
Outside - Aroys ארויס
Without - Oo'n אן
Cousin - Kuzin קוזין
Cousin - (P)Kusinkes קוזינקעס
Happy – Gliklech גליקלעך
Happy – Tsufridn צופרידן
Another/ other - Ander'e אנדערע
Side – Zayt זייט
Until – Biz ביז
Yesterday – Nachten נעכטן
Without us - Nisht mit untz נישט מיט אונז
Since - Vayl ווייל
Since - Zint זינט
Day – Toog טאג
Before – Frier פריער
Late - Shpate שפעט

But I was here until late yesterday
Ober eech bin gevain du biz shpate nachten
אבער איך בין געוועו דא ביז שפעט נעכטן

Since the other day
Zint di ander'e toog
זינט די אנדערע טאג

I want to see this in the daytime
E'ech vil zen duce bai toog
איך וויל זען דאס ביי טאג

I am happy without any of my cousins here
ikh bin tsufridn on keyn fun mayne shvesterkinder do
איך בין צופרידן אָן קיין פון מײַנע שװעסטערקינדער דאָ

Easy - Lae'echt לייכט
To find - Tsu gefinen צו געפינען
To look for/to search - Tsu ze'echen צו זיכן
To wait - Tsu varten צו ווארטן
To sell - Tsu farkoifen צו פארקויפן
To use - Tsu nitsen צו ניצן
To know - Tsu visn צו וויסן
To decide - Tsu bashlusn צו באשליסן
Both – Beyde ביידע
Night – Nacht נאכט

This place is easy to find
Duce platz iz lae'echt tsu gefinen
דאס פלאץ איז לייכט צו געפינען

I am saying to wait until tomorrow
E'ech zag tsu varten biz morgen
איך זאג צו ווארטן ביז מארגן

It's easy to sell this table
Es iz lae'echt tsu farkoyfn duce tish
עס איז לייכט צו פארקויפן דאס טיש

I want to use this
E'ech vil duce nitsen
איך וויל דאס ניצן

Where is the book?
vu iz der bukh?
ווו איז דער בוך?

I need to look for you at the mall.
ikh darf dikh zukhn in mol.
איך דארף דיך זוכן אין מאָל.

I need to be there at night
E'ech darf zayn dort ba nacht
איך דארף זיין דארט ביי נאכט

Place – Platz פלאץ
Because – Vayl ווייל
Them, they - Zey זיי
Their - Zeyer זייער
Bottle – Flashe פלאש
Mine – Mayn מיין
Myself – Zich זיך
To understand – Tsu farshteyn צו פארשטיין
Problem - Problem פראבלעם
Problems – Problemen פראבלעמען
I do, I am doing - E'ech mach איך מאך
I do, I am doing - E'ech ti איך טי
Of – Foon פון
To look - Tsu kuken צו קוקן
To do - Tsu tin צו טין
To do - Tsu ton צו טאן
Near - Leiben לעבן
Close - Nuent נאנט

Is this place near?
iz dos ort noent?
איז דאָס אָרט נאָענט?

I do what I want.
ikh tu vos ikh vil.
איך טו וואָס איך וויל.

That book is mine.
Dos iz mayn bukh
דאָס איז מײַן בוך

I need to understand the problem
E'ech darf farshteyn der problem
איך דארף פארשטיין דער פראבלעם

Enough - Genug גענוג
To buy - Tsu koyfen צו קויפֿן
Food - Essen עסען
Water - Vasser וואסער
Each/ every - Yay'den יעדן
Each/ every - Yeder יעדער
Everything - Alles אלעס
Everything - Alts אלץ
Everybody / Everyone - Yederin יעדערן
Everybody / Everyone - Alemen אלעמען
Hotel – Hotel הָאטעל

I like this hotel because it's near the beach
ikh hob lib dem hotel vayl es iz lebn dem breg
איך הָאב ליב דעם הָאטעל ווייל עס איז לעבן דעם ברעג

I want to look at the view.
ikh vil kukn afn oysblik
איך וויל קוקן אויפֿן אויסבליק.

I want to buy a bottle of water
E'ech vil koyfen a flashe vaser
איך וויל קויפֿן א פלאש וואסער

Do it like this!
tu es azoy
טו עס אזוי

Both of them have enough food
Beyde foon zey hoben genug essen
ביידע פון זיי האבן גענוג עסן

I have a view of the city from the hotel
Fin di hotel e'ech hob an oisblik foon di shtut
פון די האטעל האב איך אן אויסבליק פון די שטאט

There isn't enough time to go to Brooklyn today
Heynt iz nisht genug tseyt tsu geyn keyn bruklin
היינט איז נישט גענוג צייט צו גיין קיין ברוקלין

I like – E'ech glach איך גלייך
Family – Mishpuch'e משפחה
Parents – Eltern עלטערן
Why - Vuss וואס
Why - Far vuss פאר וואס
To say - Tsu zogn צו זאגן
Something – Epes עפעס
To go - Tsu geyn צו גיין
To work - Zu arbeiten צו ארבייטן
Who – Ver ווער
Important - Ve'echtik וויכטיג
Hello – Hi היי
What is your name? - Vus iz deyn numen? ?וואס איז דיין נאמען
Your – Deyn דיין

Hello, what is your name?
Hi, vos iz deyn nomen?
היי, וואס איז דיין נאמען?

I like to be at home with my parents
E'ech glach tsu zeyn in shtyb mit meyne eltern
איך גלייך צו זיין אין שטיב מיט מיינע עלטערן

Why do I need to say something important?
farvos darf ikh zogn epes vikhtik?
פארוואס דארף איך זאגן עפעס וויכטיק?

I am there with him
E'ech bin dort mit aim
איך בין דארט מיט עם

I like to work
E'ech glach tsu arbeiten
איך גלייך צו ארבעטן

Who is there?
Ver iz dort?
ווער איז דארט

To know - Tsu visn צו וויסן
There is - Es iz עס איז
There are - Es zenen עס זענען
Ready – Greyt גרייט
Soon – Balt באלד
That *(conjunction)* **–** Az אז
Busy – Farnumen פארנומען
How much / How many - Vi fil ווי פיל
To bring - Tsu brengen צו ברענגען
With me - Mit mir מיט מיר
Cold – Kalt קאלט
Inside – In אין

It is very cold in the library
Si zeyer kalt in der biblyotek
עס איז זייער קאלט אין דער ביבליאטעק

I am busy, but I need to be ready soon
E'ech bin farnumen, ober e'ech darf tsu zeyn greyt balt
איך בין פארנומען אבער איך דארף זיין גרייט באלד

I want to know if they are here.
ikh vil visn tsi zey zenen da.
איך וויל וויסן צי זיי זענען דא.

I can go outside.
ikh ken aroys geyen.
איך קען ארויס גיין.

There are seven dolls
Es zenen do zibn lalkes.
עס זענען דא זיבן לאלקעס

I need to know that everything is okay
E'ech darf visn az alts iz g'it
איך דארף וויסן אז אלץ איז גיט

How much money do I need to bring with me?
vifil gelt darf ikh mitbrengen?
וויפיל געלט דארף איך מיטברענגען?

Instead – Enshtot אנטשטאט
Only – Nor נאר
When – Ven ווען
I can - E'ech ken איך קען
Can I? - Ken e'ech? קען איך?
Or – Oder אדער
Were – Zenen זענען
Without me - Oo'n me'er אן מיר
To eat - Tsu essen צו עסן
To Drive - Tsu furen צו פארן
Fast – Shnel שנעל
Slow - Pamelach פּעמעלעך
Slow - Langsam לאנגזאם
Hot - Ha'ys הייס

I like bread instead of rice.
ikh hob lib broyt anshtot rayz.
איך האב ליב ברויט אנשטאט רייז

I can work today
E'ech ken arbeten haynt
איך קען ארבעטן היינט

Only when you can
Nor ven ir kent
נאר ווען איר קענט

Go there without me.
gey ahin on mir.
גיי אהין אן מיר.

I need to drive the car very fast or very slowly
E'ech darf firen di mashin zeyer shnel oder zeyer pamelach
איך דארף פירן די מאשין זייער שנעל אדער זייער פאמעלעך

I like to eat a hot meal for my lunch.
ikh hob lib tsu esn a heyse moltsayt far meyn mitog.
איך האב ליב צו עסן א הייסע מאלצייט פאר מיין מיטאג

To answer - Tsu entfern צו ענטפערן
To fly - Tsu flee'en צו פליען
To travel - Arumtsuforn ארומצופארן
To learn - Tsu lernen צו לערנען
How – Vi ווי
To leave (something) - Tsu lozn צו לאזן
To leave (a place) - Geyen גייען
Many / much - Fil פיל
A lot - Asach אסאך
I go to - E'ech gey tsu איך גיי צו
First – Ershter ערשטער
World – Velt וועלט
Synagogue - Shul שול
Around – Arim ארום
To walk - Tsu ga'yn צו גיין
Yours - deyne דיינע

Since the first time
Zint di ershter mol
זינט די ערשטע מאל

The children are yours
Di kinder zenen deyne
די קינדער זענען דיינע

I need to answer many questions
E'ech darf entfern fil shailes
איך דארף ענטפערן פיל שאלות

I want to fly today
E'ech vil flee'en haynt
איך וויל פליען היינט

You need to walk around the house
Ir darft ga'yn arum dem shtyb
איר דארפט גיין ארום דעם שטוב

To swim - Tsu shvimen צו שווימען
To practice - Tsu praktiziren צו פראקטיצירן
To play - Tsu shpiln צו שפילן
Time - Tsa'yt צייט (reference to; hour, "what time is it?")
Time - Tseyt צייט (era, moment period, duration of time)
Time – Mol מאל (occasion or frequency)
How – Vi ווי
Better – Besser בעסער

Everything is about the money.
alts iz vegn gelt.
אַלץ איז וועגן געלט.

I want to leave my dog at home.
ikh vil lozn meyn hunt in shtub.
איך וויל לאָזן מיין הונט אין שטוב.

I want to travel the world.
ikh vil arumforn di velt.
איך וויל אַרומפאָרן די וועלט.

I need to learn to swim
E'ech darf lernen tsu shvimen
איך דארף לערנען צו שווימען

I want to learn how to play better tennis.
ikh vil lernen vi tsu shpiln beser tenis.
איך וויל לערנען ווי צו שפילן בעסער טעניס.

I am going to do my homework today
Ikh gey heynt makhn meyn heymarbet
איך גיי היינט מאכן מיין היימארבעט

*With the knowledge you've gained so far, now try to create your own sentences!

Nobody - Keinemen קיינעמן
Anyone - Keyner קיינער
Against – Kegen קעגן
Us – Untz אונז
To visit - Tsu furen צו פארן
Mom / Mother – Mame מאמע
To give - Tsu gebn צו געבן
Which – Vos וואס
Just – Nor נאר
Week – Voch וואך
Than – Vi ווי
Nothing – Gornisht גארנישט

Something is better than nothing
Epes iz beser vi gornisht
עפעס איז בעסער ווי גארנישט

I am against him
E'ech bin kegen ihm
איך בין קעגן אים

Do you do this every day?
Di machst duce yeden toog?
די מאכסט דאס יעדן טאג?

We go each week to visit my family
Mir geyn yeder voch tsu bezuchen meyn mishpuch'e
מיר גיין יעדער וואך צו באזוכן מיין משפחה

I need to give you something
E'ech darf gebn ir epes
איך דארף געבן איר עפעס

*Ir is the formal "you." However, *ir* can also be used to demonstrate the indirect object pronoun of the pronoun "you," the person who is actually affected by the action that is being carried out. "I need to give you something" / *E'ech darf gebn ir epes* / איך דארף געבן איר עפעס

Towards – Tzu צו
Than – Vi ווי
To meet - Tsu trefn צו טרעפן
Someone – Emetser עמעצער
To walk - Tsu ga'yn צו גיין
Also / too / as well – Aoych אויך
Also / too / as well – Ochet אויכעט
Wednesday – Mitvoch מיטוואך
Around – Arim ארום
To drink - Tsu trinken צו טרינקען
Woman – Froe פרוי
To begin / To start – On'tsuheiben אנצוהייבן
To finish - Tsu endikn צו ענדיקן

Do you want to meet someone?
Ir vilt trefn emetser?
איר ווילט טרעפן עמעצער?

I am here also on Wednesdays
Ee'ech bin do aioch yeden mitvoch.
איך בין דא אויך יעדן מיטוואך

You need to walk around the school.
ir darft geyn arum di shule.
איר דארפֿט גיין אַרום די שולע.

We want to start the class soon.
mir viln bald onheybn dem klas.
מיר ווילן באַלד אָנהייבן דעם קלאַס.

In order to finish at three o'clock this afternoon, I need to finish soon
kdi tsu endikn dray azeyger nokh mitog, darft ikh bald endikn
כּדי צו ענדיקן דריַי אַזייגער נאָך מיטאָג, דאַרפֿט איך באַלד ענדיקן

I have - E'ech hab איך האב
Don't – Nisht נישט
Friend – Fraynd פרײנד
To borrow - Tsu borgn צו בארגן
To look like / resemble - Tsu kuken di zelba צו קוקן די זעלבע
Grandfather – Zeyde זײדע
To want - Tsu villn צו ווילן
To know - Tsu visn צו וויסן
To stay - Tsu blaybn צו בלײבן
To continue - Tsu forzetsn צו פארזעצן
Way (road, path) - Veig וועג
Way (road, path) - Strasse שטראסע
Way (road, path) - Avek אוועק
To do - Tsu tin צו טין
To do - Tsu ton צו טאן
School – shule שולע
On – Aoyf אויף

Why don't you have this book?
Farvuss hostanish duce be'yech?
פארוואס האסטו נישט דאס בוך

I want to borrow this book for my grandfather
E'ech vil borgn duce buch far meyn zeyde
איך וויל בארגן דאס בוך פאר מיין זײדע

This isn't the way to do this
Dos iz nisht der veg tsu ton dos
דאָס איז נישט דער וועג צו טאָן דאָס

I want to stay in New York because I have a friend there.
ikh vil bleybn in niu yark veyl ikh hob dort a khvr.
איך וויל בלייבן אין נעוו יארק ווייל איך האב דארט א חבר.

Our house is on the mountain.
undzer hoyz iz aoyf dem barg.
אונדזער הויז איז אויף דעם בארג.

Anyone - Keyner קיינער
To look like / resemble - Tsu kuken di zelba צו קוקן די זעלבע
I don't - E'ech (verb) nisht נישט(...) איך
To show - Tsu vayzn צו ווייזן
To prepare - Tsugreytn צוגרייטן
To come - Tsu kumen צו קומען
About - Vegn וועגן
On the - Aoyf אויף
I did not go - E'ech bin nisht gegangen איך בין נישט געגאאנגען
Do you want? - Di vilst? די ווילסט?
Correct – Re'echtik ריכטיג

Do you want to look like Arnold
Di vilst oiszehn dezelba vi Arnold?
די ווילסט אויסזען די זעלבע ווי ארנאלד

I don't want to see anyone here
E'ech vil nisht zen keinamen do
איך וויל נישט זען קיינעמען דא

I need to show you how to prepare breakfast
E'ech darf vayzn auch vi tsu greytn frishtik
איך דארף ווייזן איך ווי צו גרייטן פרישטיג

That is incorrect, I don't need the car today
Duce es nisht richdik, e'ech darf nisht di mashin haynt
דאס איז נישט ריכטיג, איך דארף נישט די מאשין היינט

I want to come with you.
Ikh vil kumen mit dir.
איך וויל קומען מיט דיר.

To remember - Tsu gedenken צו געדענקען
Your - Deyn דיין
Number – Numer נומער
Hour – Shuh שעה
Dark / darkness – Finster פינסטער
Grandmother – Bubbe באבע
Five - Fin'if פינף
Minute - Minet מינוט
More – Mehr מער
To think - Tsu trachtn צו טראכטן
To think - tracht טראכט
To hear - Tsu her'n צו הערן
Last - Let'ste לעצטע

I need to remember your number
E'ech darf gedenken deyn numer
איך דארף געדענקען דיין נומער

This is the last hour of darkness
Das iz di let'ste shoh foon fintsternish
דאס איז די לעצטע שעה פון פינצטערניש

I can hear my grandmother speaking Hebrew.
ikh ken hern mayn bobe redn hebreish.
איך קען הערן מײַן באָבע רעדן העברעיִש.

I need to think about this more.
ikh darf nokh trakhtn vegn dem.
איך דאַרף נאָך טראַכטן וועגן דעם.

From here to there, it's only five minutes
Fin do tsu dorten, es iz nor fin'if minut
פון דא צו דארטן איז נאר פינף מינוט

Again - Nochamul נאכאמאל
Again - Vider ווידער
To take - Tsu nemen צו נעמען
To try - Tsu prubirn צו פראבירן
To rent - Tsu dingen צו דינגען
Without her - Oo'n eer אן איר
To turn off – Farleshen פארלעשן
To ask - Tsu fregn צו פרעגן
To stop - Tsu oifhalten צו האלטן
Early - Frie פרי
Beach – Yam ים
Tonight - Haynt ba nacht היינט ביי נאכט

I need to try this again
E'ech darf prubirn duce nochamul
איך דארף פראבירן דאס נאכאמאל

He must go and rent a house at the beach.
er muz geyn dingen a hoyz beym breg.
ער מוז גיין דינגען א הויז ביים ברעג.

We are here for a long time
Mir zenen do far a lange tseyt
מיר זענען דא פאר א לאנגע צייט

I need to turn off the lights early tonight
E'ech darf farleshen di le'echt frie haynt ba nacht
איך דארף פארלעשן די ליכט פרי היינט ביי נאכט

We want to stop here
Mir viln oifhaltn do
מיר ווילן אויפהאלטן דא

Permission – Derloybenish דערלויבעניש
Building - Bnin בנין
Doctor - Dokter דאָקטער
Exact – Pinktlech פינקטלעך
In order to - Veigen tsu וועגן צו
Airport - Flifeld פֿליפֿעלד
Sleep - Shlofn שלאָפן
Jerusalem - Yerushalayim ירושלים
We are - Mir zenen מיר זיינען

We are from Jerusalem.
Mir zenen fun Yerushalayim.
מיר זענען פֿון ירושלים.

Your doctor is in the same building.
deyn dokter iz in der zelbiker bnin.
דיין דאָקטער איז אין דער זעלביקער בנין.

In order to leave you have to ask permission.
tsu megn geyen darft ir betn derloybenish
צו מעגן גייען דאַרפֿט איר בעטן דערלויבעניש

Is it possible to know the exact date?
Iz es meglech tsu visn di pinktleche dateh?
איז עס מעגלעך צו וויסן די פינקטלעכע דאטע?

I want to go to sleep
Ikh vil geyn shlofn
איך וויל גיין שלאָפן

Where is the airport?
Vu iz der flifeld
ווו איז דער פֿליפֿעלד?

To open - Tsu efenen צו עפענען
A bit, a little, a little bit - A'bisel א ביסל
To pay - Tsu batsulen צו באצאלן
Sister – Shvester שוועסטער
To hope - Tsu hofen צו האפן
Name – Numen נאמען
Last name - Letste numen לעצטע נאמען
Door - Ti'er טיר
To get to know - Tsu bakenin צו באקענען
Future – Tsukunft צוקונפט
To buy - Tsu koyfen צו קויפן
Nice to meet you Es iz zeir sheiine tzi trefen deir
עס איז זייער שיין צו טרעפן דיר

I need to open the door for my sister
E'ech darf tsu efenen di tiyer far meyn shvester
איך דארף עפענען די טיר פאר מיין שוועסטער

I need to buy something
E'ech darf tsu koyfn epes
איך דארף קויפן עפעס

I want to meet your brothers.
ikh vil zikh trefn mit eyere brider.
איך וויל זיך טרעפן מיט איערע ברידער.

We can hope for a better future.
mir kenen hofn aoyf a beseren tsukunft.
מיר קענען האפן אויף א בעסערען צוקונפט.

Nice to meet you, what is your name and your last name?
Es iz sheine tzi trefen deir, vos iz dein numen un deiner letste numen?
עס איז שיין צו טרעפן דיר, וואס איז דיין נאמען, און וואס איז דיין לעצטע נאמען?

To happen - Tsu gesheyen צו געשען
To live - Tsu leiben צו לעבן
To return - Tsu gayn tzurik צו גיין צוריק
There isn't – Es iz nisht עס איז נישט
There aren't – Es zenen nisht עס זענען נישט
Why - Vuss וואס
Why - Far vuss פאר וואס
Sad – Troirig טרוויריק
Happy – Gliklech גליקלעך
Excuse me - Antshuldikn mir ענטשולדיקן מיר
Children – Kinder קינדער
To order - Tsu beshtelen צו בעשטעלן

It is impossible to live without problems.
es iz aummeglekh tsu lebn on problemen.
עס איז אוממעגלעך צו לעבן אָן פראבלעמען.

I want to return to the United States.
ikh vil tsurik geyenkeyn amerike.
איך וויל צוריק גייען קיין אמעריקע.

Why are you happy right now?
Farvuss bistu tzi'friden yetst?
פארוואס ביסטו צופרידן יעצט

This needs to happen today
Duce mizz gishayen haynt
דאס מיז געשעהן היינט

Excuse me, my child is here as well
Antshuldikt mir, meyn kind iz do ochet
ענטשולדיקט מיר, מיין קינד איז דא אויכעד

I want to order a soup.
ikh vil bashteln a zup.
איך וויל באשטעלן אַ זופ.

To talk - Tsu reden צו רעדן
To speak - Shprechen צו שפרעכן
To help - Tsu helfn צו העלפן
To smoke - Tsu reychern צו רויכערן
To love - Tsu liben צו ליבן
Again - Nochamul נאכאמאל
Again - Vider ווידער
Yiddish – Yiddish יידיש
German – Deutsch דייטש
How – Vi ווי

I want to learn how to speak perfect Yiddish and German.
ikh vil lernen vi azoy tsu redn perfekte yidish aun deutsh
איך וויל לערנען ווי אזוי צו רעדן פערפֿעקטע יידיש און דײַטש

I don't want to smoke again
E'ech vil'nisht reychern nochamul
איך וויל נישט רויכערן נאכאמאל

I want to help
E'ech vil helfen
איך וויל העלפן

I love you
E'ech hob dich lib
איך האב דיך ליב

I see you
E'ech zei dir
איך זע דיר

I need you
E'ech darf dir
איך דארף דיר

*"I love you" can also be *e'ech hob dir lib*.

To read - Tsu leynen צו לייננען
To write - Tsu shrayben צו שרייבן
To teach - Tsu lernen צו לערנען
To close – Tsu far'machen צו פארמאכן
To choose - Tsu klayben צו קלייבן
To prefer - Tsu vellen beser צו וועלן בעסער
To put - Tsu ley'gn צו לייגן
To put - Tsu shteln צו שטעלן
Less – Veyniker ווייניקער
Month – Choidesh חודש
I talk - E'ech red איך רעד

I need this book to learn how to read and write in Hebrew
ikh darf dos bukh tsu lernen vi azoy tsu leyenen aun shreybn aoyf hebreish
איך דארף דאָס בוך צו לערנען ווי אזוי צו לייענען און שרייבן אויף העברעאיש

I want to teach Yiddish in Israel.
ikh vil lernen yidish in Yisroel.
איך וויל לערנען יידיש אין ישראל.

I want to turn on the lights and close the door.
ikh vil ontsindn di likht un farmakhn di tir.
איך וויל אנצינדן די ליכט און פארמאכן די טיר.

I want to pay less than you.
ikh vil batsoln veyniker vi dir.
איך וויל באצאָלן ווייניקער ווי דיר.

I prefer to put this here.
ikh vil es shteln do
איך וויל עס שטעלן דאָ

I speak with the boy and the girl in Yiddish
E'ech red mit dem yingel un di meydel oyf Yiddish
איך רעד מיט דעם יינגל און די מיידעל אויף יידיש

To exchange (*money*) - Tsu vekslen צו וועקסלען
Money – Gelt געלט
To call - Tsu rufen צו ריפן
Brother – Brider ברודער
Dad – Tate טאטע
To sit - Tsu zitsen צו זיצן
Together – Tsuzamen צוזאמען
To change - Tsu toyshen צו טוישן
During – Be'eis בעת
Years - Yu'eren יארן
Sky – Himmel הימל
Sorry – Antshuldigt ענטשולדיקט
To the – Tsu di צו די
Big – Groys גרויס
Never / ever - Keynmol קיינמאל

I am never able to exchange this money at the bank.
ikh ken keynmol nish baytn dos gelt in der bank.
איך קען קיינמאָל נישט דאָס געלט אין דער באַנק ביַיטן.

I want to call my brother and my dad today
E'ech vil rufen meyn bruder aun meyn tate haynt
איך וויל רופן מיין ברידער און מיין טאטע היינט

I am sorry.
Zay mir moykhl.
זיַי מיר מוחל

I need to put your cat on another chair
E'ech darf shteln deyn kats aoyf an andern shtul/benkel
איך דארף שטעלן דיין קאץ אויף אן אנדערן שטול/ בענקל

*This *isn't* a phrase book! The purpose of this book is *solely* to provide you with the tools to create *your own* sentences!

Up – Aroyf ארויף
Down – Aroop אראפ
Of course/certainly – Avadeh אוודאי
To follow - Tsu nochgeyn צו נאכגיין
New - Na'ye נייע
Dog - Hunt הונט
Welcome - Bruchim habaim ברוכים הבאים
Sun – Zin זין

Of course I can come to the theater, and I want to sit together with you and with your sister
Avadeh e'ech ken kimen tsum teater, aun e'ech vil zitzen tsuzamen mit deer un mit dein shvester
אוודאי קען איך קומען צו דעם טעאַטער, און איך וויל זיצן צוזאַמען מיט דיר און מיט דיין שוועסטער

If you look under the table, you can see the new rug.
aoyb ir kukt aunter dem tish, kent ir zen dem naye tepekh.
אויב איר קוקט אונטער דעם טיש, קענט איר זען דעם נייען טעפעך

I can see the sky from the window
E'ech ken zen der himmel foon di fentster
איך קען זען דער הימל פון די פענסטער

The dog wants to follow me to the store.
der hunt vil mir nochgeyen in kram.
דער הונט וויל מיר נאכגיין אין קראם

There is sun outside today.
in droysn es iz zunik haynt
אין דרויסן עס איז זוניק הײַנט.

*With the knowledge you've gained so far, now try to create your own sentences!

To allow - Tsu lozn צו לאָזן
To believe - Tsu gloyben צו גלויבן
Morning - Frii פרי
Morning - Morgen מארגן
Except – Chuts חוץ
To promise – Tsu'tsuzugen צוצוזאגן
Good night - Gutte nacht גוטע נאכט
To recognize - Tsu derkenen צו דערקענען
People – Mentshn מענטשן
Far – Vaytt ווייט
Him - Aim עם
His - Zeyn זיין
Her – Eer איר

I need to allow him to go with us.
ikh darf im lozn geyn mit aundz.
איך דארף אים לאָזן גיין מיט אונדז.

Come here quickly.
kum gikh aher.
קום גיך אַהער.

I can't recognize him.
ikh ken im nisht derkenen.
איך קען אים נישט דערקענען.

I believe everything except for this
Ikh gloyb alts akhuts dem
איך גלויב אַלץ אַחוץ דעם

I promise to say good night to my parents each night
Ikh zog tsu, tsu zogn a gute nakht tsu meyn eltern yeder nakht
איך זאָג צו צו זאָגן אַ גוטע נאַכט צו מיינע עלטערן יעדער נאַכט

Man – Mentsh מענטש
To enter - Tsu arayngein צו אריינגיין
To receive - Tsu bakumen צו באקומען
Each, every – Yeder יעדער
Good day / afternoon - Gutten tog גוטן טאג
Afternoon – Nochmitoog נאכמיטאג
Left - Links לינקס
Right - Rechts רעכטס
To move (an object) **-** Tsu riren צו רירן
To move (to a place) **–** Tsu ibergein צו איבערגיין
Different – Andersh אנדערש
I Must - E'ech mizz איך מיז

He is a different man now.
er iz itst an ander mentsh.
ער איז איצט אן אנדער מענטש.

I must move my car to the right side of the street, because my sister needs to return home this afternoon
E'ech mizz mufen meyn mashin tsu di rechte zayt foon der gass, vayl meyn shvester darf kummen tzurik aheiym haynt nachmitoog.
איך מיז מופן מיין מאשין צו די רעכטע זייט פון דער גאס ווייל מיין שוועסטער דארף קומען צוריק היינט נאכמיטאג

I see the sun in the morning from the kitchen
E'ech zeh di zin in der frieh fin di kich
איך זע די זון אין דער פרי פון די קיך

The house is on the right end of the street
Di hoyz iz aoyf di rekht suf fun di gas
די הויז איז אויף די רעכטע זייט פון די גאס

To wish - Tsu vintshen צו ווינטשן
Bad – Shlecht שלעכט
To get - Tsu bakumen צו באקומען
To forget - Tsu fargesen צו פארגעסן
Everybody / Everyone - Yederin יעדערן
Everybody / Everyone - Alemen אלעמען
Although – Chotsh כאטש
To feel - Tsu filn צו פילן
Great – Groys גרויס
To like - Tsu glaichen צו גלייכן
In front – Forent אין פארענט
Past – Fargangenhayt פארגאנגענהייט

I don't want to wish anything bad
E'ech vil nisht vintshn epes shlecht
איך וויל נישט ווינטשן עפעס שלעכטס

I must forget everybody from my past.
ikh muz fargesn alemen fun meyn fargangenheyt.
איך מוז פארגעסן אלעמען פון מיין פארגאנגענהייט.

To feel well I must take vitamins
tsu filn gezunt muz ikh nemen vitamins
צו פילן געזונט מוז איך נעמען וויטאַמינס

I am next to the person behind you
E'ech bin noent tsu di mentsh hinter dir
איך בין נאנט צו די מענטש הינטער דיר

There is a person in front of me
Es iz duh a mentsh in forent fin mir
עס איז דא א מענטש אין פארענט פון מיר

I go into the house from the front entrance and not through the yard.
ikh gey areyn in hoyz fun di fodishten arayngang un nisht durkh di hoyf.
איך גיי אריין אין די הויז פון די פֿאָדישטען אַרײַנגאַנג און נישט דורך די הויף.

Next (following, after) — Vayter ווייטער
Next (near, close) — Nuent נאנט
Behind — Hinter הינטער
Well (as in doing well) — Gutt גוט
Restaurant — Restoran רעסטאראן
Bathroom — Klozet קלאזעט
Goodbye (be well) — Zai gezunt זיי געזונט

Goodbye my friend.
zay gezunt meyn fraynd.
זײַ געזונט מיין פרײַנד.

Which is the best restaurant in the area?
vos iz der bester restoran in der gegnt?
װאָס איז דער בעסטער רעסטאָראַן אין דער געגנט?

I can feel the heat.
ikh ken filn di hits.
איך קען פילן די היץ.

I need to repair a part of the cabinet of the bathroom.
ikh darf farikhtn a teyl fun di kabinet fun di klozet.
איך דאַרף פאַריכטן אַ טייל פון די קאַבינעט פון די קלאָזעט.

I want a car before next year
ikh vil a mashin fahr dem kummendiker yor
איך וויל אַ מאַשין פאַר דעם קומענדיקער יאר

I like the house, but it is very small.
ikh hob lib dem hoyz, ober es iz zeyer kleyn.
איך האָב ליב דעם הויז, אָבער עס איז זייער קליין.

*"Bathroom" is *klozet*. (It can mean "closet" as well.)

Please - Bit'e ביטע
To remove / to take out - Tsu nemen aroys צו נעמען ארויס
Beautiful – Sheyn שיין
To lift - Tsu heyben צו הייבן
Include / Including – Einshlissen איינשליסן
Belong – Geheren געהערן
To check - Tsu kontrolirn צו קאנטראלירן
Small – Kleyn קליין

She wants to remove this door, please
Zi vil aveknemen dem ti'er, bit'e
זי וויל אוועקנעמען דעם טיר, ביטע

We need to check the size of the house
Mir darfen kontrolirn di greys foon der hoyz
מיר דארפן קאנטראלירן די גרויס פון דער הויז

I want to lift this.
ikh vil das aoyfheybn.
איך וויל דאס אויפהייבן.

Can you please put the wood in the fire?
kent ir bite shteln di holts in di fayer?
קענט איר ביטע שטעלן די האָלץ אין די פייַער?

This doesn't belong here, I need to check again
Duce gehert nisht do, e'ech darf vider kontrolirn
דאס געהערט נישט דא, איך דארף ווידער קאנטראלירן

Where is the synagogue?
Vu iz der shul
ווּ איז דער שול

Real - Praktish פראקטיש
Real - Faktish פאקטיש
Weather – Veter וועטער
Size – Groys גרויס
High – Hoych הויך
Doesn't – Nisht נישט
So – Azoy אזוי
Price – Prayz פרייז
To hold - Tsu halten צו האלטן
Hospital - Shpitol שפּיטאָל
Expensive – Tayer טייער

Is that a real diamond?
iz dos an emese diamant?
איז דאָס אַן אמתע דיאמענט?

This week the weather was very beautiful
Diy voch di veter iz geven zeyer sheyn
די וואך די וועטער איז געווען זייער שיין

I can pay this although the price is expensive
E'ech ken batsoln duce chotsh der prayz iz tayer
איך קען דאס באצאלן כאטש דער פרייז איז טייער

Can you please hold my hand?
Kenstu bite haltn meyn hant?
קענצו ביטע האַלטן מיין האַנט?

Where is the hospital?
Vau iz der shpitol?
וואו איז דער שפּיטאָל?

The sun is high in the sky.
di zun iz hoykh in himl.
די זון איז הויך אין הימל.

Building Bridges

In Building Bridges, we take six conjugated verbs that have been selected after studies I have conducted for several months in order to determine which verbs are most commonly conjugated, and which are then automatically followed by an infinitive verb. For example, once you know how to say, "I need," "I want," "I can," and "I like," you will be able to connect words and say almost anything you want more correctly and understandably. The following three pages contain these six conjugated verbs in first, second, third, fourth, and fifth person, as well as some sample sentences. Please master the entire program up until here prior to venturing onto this section.

I want - E'ech vil איך וויל / **I need -** E'ech darf איך דארף
I can - E'ech ken איך קען
I like - E'ech glach איך גלייך
I go - E'ech gey איך גיי
I have - E'ech hob איך האב
I must / I have to - E'ech mizz איך מיז

I want to go to my apartment
E'ech vil geyn tsu meyn voynung
איך וויל גיין צו מיין וואונונג

I can go with you to the bus station
E'ech ken geyn mit ir tsu di oytobus stantsye
איך קען גיין מיט דיר צו די אויטאבוס סטאנציע

I need to leave the museum.
ikh darf avek geyen fun der muzeum.
איך דארף אוועקגייען פון דער מוזייאום

I like to eat oranges.
ikh hob lib tsu esn marantsn.
איך האָב ליב צו עסן מאַראַנצן.

I am going to teach a class
E'ech ga'i lernen a klas
איך גיי לערנען א קלאס

I have to speak to my teacher
E'ech mizz reden tsu meyn lerer
איך מיז רעדן צו מיין לערער

Please master *every* single page up until here prior to attempting the following two pages!

You want - Di vilst די ווילסט

Do you want? - Vilstu? ?ווילסטו

He wants - Er vil ער וויל

Does he want? - Vil er? ?וויל ער

She wants - Zi vil זי וויל

Does she want? - Tut zi velen? ?טוט זי וועלן

We want - Mir vilen מיר ווילן

Do we want? - Tu'en mir vilen? ?טוען מיר וועלן

They want - Zey vilen זיי ווילן

Do they want? - Tu'en zey velen? ?טוען זיי וועלן

You (plural) want – Ir vilt איר ווילט

Do you (plural) want? – Vilt ir? ?ווילט איר

You need - Ir darft איר דארפט

Do you need? - Darft ir? ?דארפט איר

He needs - Er darf ער דארף

Does he need? - Tut er darfen? ?טוט ער דארפן

She needs - Zi darf זי דארף

Does she need? - Tut zi darfen? ?טוט זי דארפן

They need - Zey darfen זיי דארפן

Do they need? - Tu'en zey darfen? ?טוען זיי דארפן

You (plural) need – Ir darft איר דארפט

You can - Ir kent איר קענט

Can you? - Kent ir? ?קענט איר

He can - Er ken ער קען

Can he? - Ken er? ?קען ער

She can Zi ken זי קען

Can she? - Ken zi? ?קען זי

We can - Mir kenin מיר קענען

Can we? - Kenin mir? ?קענען מיר

They can Zey kenin זיי קענען

Can they? - Kenin zey? ?קענען זיי

You (plural) can – Ir kent איר קענט

You like - Di glaichst די גלייכסט

Do you like? - Glaichstu? ?גלייכסטו

He likes Er glaicht ער גלייכט

Does he like? - Tut er glaichen? ?טוט ער גלייכן

She likes - Zi glaicht זי גלייכט

Does she like? - Tut zi glaichen? ?טוט זי גלייכן

We like - Mir glaichen מיר גלייכן

Do we like? - Tu'en mir glaichen? ?טוען מיר גלייכן

They like - Zey glaichen זיי גלייכן

Do they like? - Tu'en zey glaichen? ?טוען זיי גלייכן

You (plural) like – Ir glaicht איר גלייכט

You go - Di geyst די גייסט

Do you go? - Tistu geyn? טיסטו גיין?

He goes - Er geyt ער גייט

Does he go? - Tut er geyn? טוט ער גיין?

She goes - Zi geyt זי גייט

Does she go? - Tut zi geyn? טוט זי גיין?

We go - Mir geyen מיר גיין

Do we go? - Tu'en mir geyn? טוען מיר גיין?

They go - Zey geyn זיי גיין

Do they go? - Tu'en zey geyn? טוען זיי גיין?

You (plural) go – Ir geht איר גייט

You have - Di hostz די האסט

Do you have? - Tsi hostu? צו האסטו?

He has - Er hott ער האט

Does he have? - Tut er hobn? טוט ער האבן?

She has - Zi hott זי האט

Does she have? - Tut zi hobn? טוט זי האבן?

We have - Mir hobn מיר האבן

Do we have? - Tu'en mir hobn? טוען מיר האבן?

They have - Zey hobn זיי האבן

Do they have? - Tu'en zey hobn? טוען זיי האבן?

You (plural) have - Alle hoben אלע האבן

Do you want to go?
Di vilst geyn?
די ווילסט גיין?

He wants to fly
Er vil fli'en
ער וויל פליען

We want to swim
Mir vilen shvimen
מיר ווילן שווימען

Do they want to run?
Tsu vilen zey loyfen?
צו ווילן זיי לויפן?

Do you need to clean?
Di darfst romen?
די דארפסט רוימען?

She needs to sing a song
Zi darf zingen a lid
זי דארף זינגען א ליד

We need to travel
Mir darfen arumtsuforn
מיר דארפן ארומצופארן

They don't need to fight
Zey darfen zich nisht tsukreygn
זיי דארפן זיך נישט צוקריגן

You (plural) need to save your money.
ir (plural) muzt shporn aier gelt.
איר מיזט שפארן אייער געלט

Can you hear me?
Di kenst mich hern?
די קענסט מיך הערן?

He can dance very well
Er ken tantsn zeyer gut
ער קען טאנצן זייער גוט

214

We can go out tonight
Mir kenen aroysgeyn haynt ba nacht
מיר קענען ארויסגיין היינט ביינאכט

During an emergency, firefighters can break down a door.
Fayerleshers kenen tsubrekhn a tir beshas a noytfal.
פֿײַערלעשערס קענען צוברעכן אַ טיר בשעת אַ נויטפֿאַל

Do you like to eat here?
Ir glaicht tsu esn do?
איר גלייכט צו עסן דא?

He likes to spend time here
Er glaicht tsu farbrengen tseyt do
איר גלייכט צו פארברענגען צייט דא

We like to fix the house
Mir glaichen zu reparyeren dem shtyb
מיר גלייכן צו רעפארירן דעם שטיב

They like to cook
Zey glaichen tsu kochen
זיי גלייכן צו קאכן

You (plural) like to play soccer.
ir (plural) hot lib tsu shpiln fusbol.
איר האָט ליב צו שפילן פוסבאָל.

Do you go to the movies on weekends?
Geyt ir in kino sof vokh?
גייט איר אין קינאָ סוף וואך?

He goes fishing
Er geyt khapen fish
ער גייט כאפן פיש

We are going to see the moon
Mir gehen zen di levuna
מיר גען זען די לבנה

They go out to eat at a restaurant every day.
zey geyn esn in a restoran yeden tog.
זיי גיין עסן אין אַ רעסטאָראַן יעדן טאג

Do you have money?
Tsi hott ir gelt?
צו האט איר געלט?

He needs to go to sleep
Er darf geyn shlofn
ער דארף גיין שלאפן

She must look outside
Zi mizz kiken aroys
זי מוז קיקן ארויס

We must sign our names
Mir mizzen shrayben unzer nemen
מיר מוזן שרייבן אונזער נעמען

They must send the letter
Zey mizzen shikn dem briv
זיי מוזן שיקן דעם בריוו

You (plural) have to stand in line.
ir (plural) muzt shteyn in a rey.
איר מוזט שטיין אין אריי

Other Useful Tools in the Yiddish Language

Months - Chodoshim חדשים
January – Yanuar יאַנואַר
February – Februar פֿעברואַר
March – Marts מאַרץ
April – April אַפּריל
May – May מײַ
June – Yuni יוני
July – Yuli יולי
August – Oygust אויגוסט
September – September סעפּטעמבער
October – Oktober אָקטאָבער
November – November נאָוועמבער
December – Detsember דעצעמבער

Directions – **Instruktsyes** אינסטרוקציעס
North – Tsofn צפון
South – Darum דרום
East – Mizrach מזרח
West – Mariv מעריב

Days of the Week - Teg foon der voch טעג פֿון דער וואָך
Sunday – Zuntik זונטיק
Monday – Montik מאָנטיק
Tuesday – Dinstig דינסטיק
Wednesday – Mitvoch מיטוואָך
Thursday – Donershtig דאָנערשטיק
Friday – Freytig פֿרײַטיק
Saturday – Shabes שבת

Seasons – **Tseytn** צייטן
Spring - Friling פֿרילינג
Summer – Zumer זומער
Autumn – Harbst האַרבסט
Winter – Vinter ווינטער

Colors – Kolieren קאלירן
Black – Shvarts שוואַרץ
White - Veyse ווײַס
Blue – Bloy בלאָ
Yellow – Gale געל
Green – Grin גרין
Orange – Marants מאַראַנץ
Purple – Lila לילאַ
Brown – Broynברוין
Pink - Roz ראָז

Numbers – Numern נומערן
One – Eyns איינס
Two – Tsvey צוויי
Three – Drey דרײַ
Four – Fir פיר
Five – ind פינף
Six – Zeks זעקס
Seven – Zibn זיבן
Eight – Acht אכט
Nine – Neyn נײַן
Ten – Tsen צען
Twenty – Tsvantsik צוואַנציק
Thirty – Draysik דרײַסיק
Forty – Fertsik פערציק
Fifty – Fuftsik פופציק
Sixty – Zekhtsik זעכציק
Seventy – Zibetsik זיבעציק
Eighty – Akhtsik אַכציק
Ninety – Nayntsik נײַנציק
Hundred – Hundert הונדערט
Thousand – Toyznt טויזנט
Million – Milyon מיליאָן

Conclusion

Congratulations! You have completed all the tools needed to master the German, Dutch, Danish, Norwegian, Swedish and Yiddish, and I hope that this has been a valuable learning experience. Now you have sufficient communication skills to be confident enough to embark on a visit a Germanic speaking country, impress your friends, and boost your resume so *good luck*.

This program is available in other languages as well, and it is my fervent hope that my language learning programs will be used for good, enabling people from all corners of the globe and from all cultures and religions to be able to communicate harmoniously. After memorizing the required three hundred and fifty words, please perform a daily five-minute exercise by creating sentences in your head using these words. This simple exercise will help you grasp conversational communications even more effectively. Also, once you memorize the vocabulary on each page, follow it by using a notecard to cover the words you have just memorized and test yourself and follow *that* by going back and using this same notecard technique on the pages you studied during the previous days. This repetition technique will assist you in mastering these words in order to provide you with the tools to create your own sentences.

Every day, use this notecard technique on the words that you have just studied.

Everything in life has a catch. The catch here is just consistency. If you just open the book, and after the first few pages of studying the program, you put it down, then you will not gain anything. However, if you consistently dedicate a half hour daily to studying, as well as reviewing what you have learned from previous days, then you will quickly realize why this method is the most effective technique ever created to become conversational in a foreign language. My technique works! For anyone who doubts this technique, all I can say is that it has worked for me and hundreds of others.

Congratulations! Now You Are on Your Own!

If you merely absorb the required three hundred and fifty words in this book, you will then have acquired the basis to become conversational in the Germanic languages! After memorizing these three hundred and fifty words, this conversational foundational basis that you have just gained will trigger your ability to make improvements in conversational fluency at an amazing speed! However, in order to engage in quick and easy conversational communication, you need a special type of basics, and this book will provide you with just that.

Unlike the foreign language learning systems presently used in schools and universities, along with books and programs that are available on the market today, that focus on *everything* but being conversational, *this* method's sole focus is on becoming conversational in a foreign language. Once you have successfully mastered the required words in this book, there are two techniques that if combined with these essential words, can further enhance your skills and will result in you improving your proficiency tenfold. *However*, these two techniques will only succeed *if* you have completely and successfully absorbed the three hundred and fifty words. *After* you establish the basis for fluent communications by memorizing these words, you can enhance your conversational abilities even more if you use the following two techniques.

The first step is to attend a language class (in whichever one of these languages which you just mastered) that will enable you to sharpen your grammar. You will gain additional vocabulary and learn past and present tenses, and if you apply these skills that you learn in the class, together with the three hundred and fifty words that you have previously memorized, you will be improving your conversational skills tenfold. You will notice that, conversationally, you will succeed at a much higher rate than any of your classmates. A simple second technique is to choose foreign subtitles while watching a movie. If you have successfully mastered and grasped these three hundred and fifty words, then the combination of the two—those words along with the subtitles—will aid you considerably in putting all the grammar into perspective, and again, conversationally, you will improve tenfold.

Once you have established a basis of quick and easy conversation in these 3 languages with those words that you just attained, every additional word or grammar rule you pick up from there on will be gravy. And these additional words or grammar rules can be combined with the three hundred and fifty words, enriching your conversational abilities even more. Basically, after the research and studies I've conducted with my method over the years, I came to the conclusion that in order to become conversational, you first must learn the words and *then* learn the grammar.

The languages featured in this book are compatible with the mirror translation technique. Likewise, with *this* language, you can use this mirror translation technique in order to become conversational, enabling you to communicate even more effortlessly. Mirror translation is the method of translating a phrase or sentence, word for word from English to another foreign language, by using these imperative words that you have acquired through this program (such as the sentences I used in this book). Latin languages, Middle Eastern languages, and Slavic languages, along with a few others, are also compatible with the mirror translation technique. Though you won't be speaking Shakespearean, you will still be fully understood and, conversation-wise, be able to get by just fine.

NOTE FROM THE AUTHOR

Thank you for your interest in my work. I encourage you to share your overall experience of this book by posting a review. Your review can make a difference! Please feel free to describe how you benefited from my method or provide creative feedback on how I can improve this program. I am constantly seeking ways to enhance the quality of this product, based on personal testimonials and suggestions from individuals like you. In order to post a review, please check with the retailer of this book.

Thanks and best of luck,
Yatir Nitzany

www.ingramcontent.com/pod-product-compliance
Lightning Source LLC
Chambersburg PA
CBHW070135080526
44586CB00015B/1708